Copyright

M000119160

100 Days: The rush to judgment that killed Nortel
© 2013 by James Bagnall

Published by the Ottawa Citizen.

OTTAWA CITIZEN

The Ottawa Citizen

1101 Baxter Road

Ottawa, Ontario, Canada

K2C 3M4

About the Author

James Bagnall, the Associate Business Editor at The Ottawa Citizen, has been reporting on business since 1978. He began his career at The Financial Post and The Financial Times of Canada before joining the Citizen in 1993.

Bagnall has won multiple business writing awards including a National Newspaper Award in 2013 for his coverage of Nortel Networks' descent into ruin.

The author has travelled widely in pursuit of stories during his lengthy career. He has organized and written special reports on South Africa, India, Israel, Germany and Britain, and has reported extensively on the federal government of Canada and its many agencies and departments.

Bagnall graduated in 1975 from University of Toronto's Trinity College, where he also served as Chairman of the Joint Board of Stewards.

Table of Contents

100 Days
The rush to judgment that killed Nortel

Foreword

I've had the good fortune over the years to interview hundreds of talented, unusual individuals who worked at Nortel Networks in an astonishing array of jobs and locations. Nearly every one of them still feels the pain of what was lost in 2009 when this telecommunications legend fell into bankruptcy, never to emerge. A few years ago, I wrote the story of how Nortel had failed as a business. But it was clear there was more to be told.

Something profound had been buried in the extraordinary circumstances of 2004, when Nortel's directors sacked their top three financial executives. The company had been so close to clawing its way back to health, then lost its momentum after a host of outside investigators took control of the company's agenda.

The story of Nortel's demise is as much a legal one as it is a business tale. However, the ongoing litigation inhibited potential sources from speaking out. It wasn't until 2012 that a yearlong criminal trial in Toronto threw open a window into some of Nortel's most secret deliberations. The public could finally begin to discern the real shape of the corporate tragedy that unfolded.

Not all the answers were tendered in Judge Frank Marrocco's courtroom. Important deliberations took place in Washington, D.C., Brampton, Ont. and on Bay Street. The crux is that flawed conclusions were reached about Nortel's accounting that the 2012 trial determined were unwarranted – and no one challenged the initial rush to judgment. This book attempts to explain how the stewards of a century-old enterprise let it happen. While this is almost entirely an original work, some parts of the text incorporate material from columns that previously appeared in the Ottawa Citizen.

Many members of the former Nortel community helped shaped my perspective for this project, but the shadow of continuing civil litigation prompted many to request anonymity. I would normally thank those who don't mind being named, but that would make it easier to identify the others. I am immensely thankful for their assistance with many aspects of this rather complicated saga. I am grateful, too, for the patience shown by a few experts who accepted my requests for clarification again and again. I hope they find I have interpreted them correctly.

I am in debt to my employer, the Ottawa Citizen, for allowing me to consume months of staff time to work nearly exclusively on this project. I especially appreciated the encouragement of Gerry Nott, publisher and editor-in-chief, and Andrew Potter, managing editor. And, not least, my colleague Christine Brousseau spent considerable effort amid her regular duties shaping the final product, giving it much greater clarity and readability.

Dedication

To Sharon, for a life, and the lessons of Davlins Drift.

Cast of characters:

Prelude

The independent investigators and the lawyers who invited them in:

William McLucas, a partner with Wilmer Cutler Pickering Hale and Dorr LLP, the Washington-based law firm hired in 2003 by Nortel's audit committee to provide a second opinion on the company's restatement. McLucas is a former director of investigations for the U.S. Securities and Exchange Commission.
Laura Wertheimer, the lead investigator on the Nortel file for Wilmer Cutler.
David Becker, a former counsel with the SEC. Becker suggested the idea of hiring Wilmer Cutler.
Stephen Burlone, a partner with Huron Consulting, the forensic firm hired by Wilmer Cutler to provide advice on accounting.
Nicholas DeRoma, the Nortel in-house lawyer who recommended Wilmer Cutler to the board of directors.

The 2012 trial

The accused:

Frank Dunn, the chief executive officer of Nortel Networks from November 2001 to April 2004. He joined Nortel's finance group in 1976.
Douglas Beatty, the chief financial officer of Nortel Networks from July 2002 to April 2004.
Michael Gollogly, controller of Nortel Networks from July 2002 to April 2004.

The judge:

Frank Marrocco, a onetime prosecutor and former partner with Gowlings who was appointed to the bench of the Ontario Superior Court in 2005.
The Crown:

Robert Hubbard, the chief prosecutor who joined the case in 2009 after winning a fraud conviction against Garth Drabinsky and Marvin Gottlieb, principals of the Toronto theatre production company Livent.
David Friesen, Crown attorney who in 2011 secured a fraud conviction against Robert Waxman, a prominent Hamilton businessman.
Amanda Rubaszek, part of Hubbard's team in the Drabinsky, Gottlieb trial.
Sandy Tse, the Crown attorney who handled the Nortel file early on.

The RCMP:

Rafael Alvarado, the computer expert who organized the Nortel document database.
Debbie Bone, the first investigator assigned to the case.
Kevin Burk, investigator.
Brian Butler, the agency's accounting guru at trial.
John Shoemaker, investigator.

The Defence:

For Frank Dunn:

David Porter, the partner with McCarthy Tétrault who led the defence arguments at trial.
Sarit Batner, partner with McCarthy Tétrault.

John Dent, independent lawyer and former McCarthy Tétrault litigation associate.
Andrew Matheson, partner with McCarthy Tétrault.
Harry Underwood, the partner with McCarthy Tétrault who cross-examined the most hostile Crown witnesses.

For Douglas Beatty:

Gregory Lafontaine, independent lawyer and principal of Lafontaine & Associates.
Lori Anne Thomas, associate lawyer, Lafontaine & Associates.

For Michael Gollogly:

Sharon Lavine, partner with Greenspan Humphrey Lavine.
Robin McKechney, partner with Greenspan Humphrey Lavine.

The witnesses from Nortel:

John Cleghorn, the chairman of the audit committee who hired Wilmer Cutler to provide a second opinion on Nortel's first restatement.
Ken Crosson, vice-president of global operations and the only one of Nortel's five business unit leaders to testify.
Peter Dans, director of financial planning from June 2003.
Brian Harrison, director of financial planning until June 2003. The Crown's lead witness, Harrison testified about Nortel's use of forecasting and how this allegedly influenced accounting decisions.

Bill Kerr, vice-president of finance after Beatty was placed on leave March 15, 2004.

Jim Kinney, vice-president of finance for wireless and the only one of Nortel's five finance vice-presidents to testify.

Michael McMillan, director of consolidations starting in January 2003.

Linda Mezon, assistant corporate controller who reported to Beatty.

Glenn Morita, director of finance for Nortel's European/Asian region.

Sue Shaw, manager of consolidations and author of the "303 document."

Karen Sledge, U.S. controller during the first three sets of financial statements for 2002 and 2003.

Helen Verity, director of consolidations until January 2003.

Red Wilson, chairman of Nortel's board of directors.

Other witnesses:

Don Hathway, Deloitte partner with lead responsibility for the U.S. audit.

Thomas Heintzman, a McCarthy Tétrault partner who was called upon to testify about a meeting between his client, Dunn, and the investigators from Wilmer Cutler.

Bruce Richmond, Deloitte partner with responsibility for managing the Nortel account.

Junior Sirivar, McCarthy Tétrault associate who also attended the meeting between Dunn and Wilmer Cutler.

Other key characters

Jeff Ansley, Assistant U.S. Attorney in 2008 for the Northern District of Texas. Ansley decided not to pursue criminal charges against Dunn, Beatty or Gollogly.

Cary Boswell, the Ontario Superior Court Justice who ruled in 2009 the accused must be able to search the full database of evidence.

Bob Brown, member of Nortel's board of directors.

Colin Campbell, the Ontario Superior Court Justice who ruled Chubb Insurance was within its rights to deny coverage for half the legal expenses incurred by Dunn and Beatty. Campbell was overruled by the Court of Appeal.

John Cawthorne, the Deloitte partner with signing authority for Nortel's financial statements. He was scheduled to testify but the Crown pulled him as a witness at the last minute.

Robert Chambers, the Crown's accounting expert. He wasn't called as a witness.

Clarence Chandran, former chief operating officer of Nortel. He had been selected to succeed John Roth as CEO but bowed out due to illness, making way for Dunn.

Richard Clarke, the Deloitte partner who was replaced, as part of a regular rotation, on the Nortel account by Cawthorne.

Ian Craig, a former chief marketing officer at Nortel who retired in 2000.

Jim Goodfellow, the Deloitte partner who had been selected to replace Hathway until the Wilmer Cutler investigation intervened.

Robert Ingram, one of three Nortel directors present at Dunn's firing.

Greg Mumford, the head of Nortel's optical products group in 2001.

Bill Owens, the board member who took over as CEO after Dunn was fired in 2004.

John Roth, a former CEO of Nortel who retired in 2001.

Mitch Szorcsik, the Deloitte partner who preceded Hathway. Szorcsik and Clarke signed off on Nortel's accounts twice before Wilmer Cutler arrived on the scene.

Mike Zafirovski, Nortel's CEO from 2005 to 2009.

Prologue

Three Men in a Cell

Dawn broke early over metropolitan Toronto on June 19, 2008, revealing a thick cover of clouds. Three men in their fifties, all former executives of Nortel Networks, were beginning their day in different parts of the city. They had braced themselves to endure the events about to unfold.

Frank Dunn, the former CEO of the country's largest high-tech firm, answered a knock at the door of his waterfront home along Oakville's millionaires' row. There, as prearranged, was David Porter, a partner with McCarthy Tétrault. The Toronto corporate lawyer had been helping Dunn prepare his defence and would eventually play a leading role at trial. But on this day, Porter was to escort his client to an RCMP detachment in Newmarket, just north of Toronto.

A few kilometres to the west of Dunn's house, Nortel's former top accountant, Michael Gollogly, was already getting into his car. Despite their physical proximity, Gollogly and Dunn never saw each other –

they did not get along. Gollogly and his wife, Mary, left for Newmarket around 6:30 a.m. and were the first to arrive at the RCMP facility. There, they were joined by Douglas Beatty, the former chief financial officer who lived just a 30-minute drive south of the detachment and, eventually, Dunn.

The police were civil. "This may look weird," said one officer, "but I have to actually touch you." It was part of the arresting procedure. He tapped each suspect on the shoulder and read out seven charges – later reduced to two – involving fraud against the public and deliberate misrepresentation of Nortel's financial results. The businessmen were fingerprinted and photographed, then led to a cell. There was one for each of them. They had solid walls but no bars and the doors were kept open. Someone asked if they wanted water.

The mood changed when it came time for the transfer to the nearby Newmarket courthouse. "Arms behind your back," the constable said. The handcuffs went on. A moment of disbelief as the accused suddenly realized what was happening. Dunn, Beatty and Gollogly were escorted to a minivan by three policemen. They entered the courthouse by the basement. Their cuffs were removed to be replaced by another set, but now their hands were in front.

The former executives walked up the stairs where they saw several large cells. These were solid concrete block enclosures, with steel bars on the front. A constable directed them into an empty one. They were to wait there until their lawyers arranged bail. To kill the tension, Dunn and Beatty talked sports. Gollogly kept mostly to himself. They had not seen each other since April 2004, when Nortel's board of directors had fired them 'for cause.' The directors had never explained the cause with any precision. The RCMP wasn't much more specific.

After the lawyers posted bail, the accused were free to go. Gollogly walked out, head down. He knew the media would be there in force and had arranged to meet Mary – like him, a former Nortel employee – in a nearby café. Dunn was accompanied by his wife, Nancy, and their daughter Kelly. The former CEO was angry, defiant, but he listened to his lawyer, who counselled silence.

Beatty escaped attention even though he exited the courthouse right after Dunn. The former CFO was accompanied by his brother, who at six-foot-three looked like a policeman. The siblings walked right through the media horde and no one recognized them. For years to come, while the Crown prepared its case, the images of an angry Dunn and a subdued Gollogly would appear in the media again and again. For Beatty, news organizations had to make do with a picture of a smiling corporate executive – a file shot from better days.

§

Nowhere in the RCMP's synopsis of its case that day was there an explanation for what, exactly, was wrong with the way the accused had handled their firm's accounting. The RCMP had rotated several investigators through the case in the past four years, yet none seemed to have grasped the complexity of Nortel's books.

The charges were vague: The former executives stood accused of manipulating their company's accounts to produce desired earnings, of knowingly misrepresenting Nortel's financial health to the investing public, and of profiting personally by accepting millions of dollars' worth of executive bonuses. Such allegations were practically meaningless because everything rests in the details – in the assumptions used to justify the relevant accounting entries. The RCMP had little to say about these.

The accused knew they had done nothing improper. But it would be another four-and-a-half years before an independent outsider with real power – Ontario Superior Court Justice Frank Marrocco – would confirm their innocence.

Marrocco rendered his verdict in a judgment so tightly argued that the Crown declined to appeal. Yet, bizarrely, there was a sense in many parts of the country that somehow Nortel's top financial guns had gotten away with something.

A Queen's University business professor suggested the day of Marrocco's ruling that if the Crown's lawyers had been better trained in advanced accounting, a guilty verdict might have been easier to secure. Social media feeds were full of comments decrying the 'separate' standard of justice for defendants such as Dunn, who could afford the finest Bay Street lawyers. Other commenters suggested that had this been a civil fraud trial – with its lower burden of proof – then the judgment would have been very different.

Not least, following Nortel's demise, in which shareholders, employees and pensioners all suffered significant financial losses, there was a widely held view that someone should pay. The accused had been served up by the company itself, by the RCMP and by the Crown. They had been targeted by the Ontario Securities Commission and the U.S. Securities and Exchange Commission. For nearly a decade, Dunn, Beatty and Gollogly had borne the public's anger over what had been lost.

But now an Ontario judge had determined that these were not the guys. Indeed, Marrocco declared there had been no crime – that a host of investigators and overseers had reached the wrong conclusions about what had driven the accounting decisions at Nortel. In too many quarters his was a deeply unpopular, even disturbing, ruling.

The accused knew it. The instant they heard Marrocco pronounce "charges dismissed," Dunn, Beatty and Gollogly showed relief, not exuberance. It had been their misfortune to be in charge of Nortel's books during an extraordinary confluence of circumstance and events. In private moments, with friends they could trust, they had shared the incredible story of what had transpired – the story of how Nortel's board of directors, the stewards of a century-old enterprise, had meekly accepted the hurried findings of an independent investigator and then cut them adrift.

Dunn, Beatty and Gollogly hoped that once the facts emerged, people would finally understand the depth of the injustice that had been meted out. But they knew equally that many people, perhaps most, wouldn't care. The company was ruined.

Nortel had been a symbol of Canada's entrepreneurial brilliance – a corporation that once hired one of every three of the country's advanced electrical engineering grads and sold advanced communications gear to customers in more than 100 countries. Nortel's engineers had won a global race to build the fastest, most stable optical networks ever deployed. In 2000, at the height of the telecom boom, these technical marvels carried 70 per cent of the globe's Internet traffic – a feat celebrated in a famous ad featuring the Beatles' classic, Come Together.

But at its moment of supreme triumph, Nortel failed the most basic job of due diligence – to dig more deeply into its customers' order books to discern the weakness in its position. Its top managers, blinded by hubris and the speed of their journey, missed the signs that would have told them their world was changing. It was this failure, not fraud, that was at the root of the accounting mess that plagued the company until the day it vanished.

1

An Epiphany in Raleigh-
Durham

There was a peculiar mood that day, everyone noticed it. Early in February 2001, a dozen or so executives gathered in a boardroom at Nortel Networks' regional headquarters on the outskirts of Raleigh-Durham, N.C. Led by chief operating officer Clarence Chandran, the sales executive slated to take over as CEO later that spring, they were to review company operations and prospects.

Just three weeks earlier Nortel had announced a record $30 billion in sales for 2000 and CEO John Roth predicted this would jump another $10 billion in 2001. (All figures U.S. except where indicated.) The forecast surprised industry skeptics and some of Nortel's less senior managers – the ones closest to the customers. But it hadn't been conjured up from thin air. It was based on intelligence supplied by the people in the room, most notably Greg Mumford, the head of Nortel's optical products group.

Mumford's business unit, with $10 billion in revenues the previous year, had been struggling to keep up with orders from customers such as Qwest Communications of Denver and MCI Communications of Washington, D.C.

These and dozens of smaller carriers were building fibre-optic networks at breakneck pace to win over a new generation of subscribers with high-speed Internet services. They had assured Mumford throughout the fourth quarter and into January that they would continue buying optical gear at prodigious rates. Indeed, one customer demanded that Mumford sell it transmission gear that had already been allocated to one of the customer's rivals. Mumford refused.

There were a few worrying signs. Some customers had warehouses stuffed full of Nortel technology still waiting to be deployed. But when queried about their ability to absorb more, the customers responded: "Let us worry about that, just keep our place in your production line."

Other hints something was amiss could be discerned by the public. Three-and-a-half months before the meeting in Raleigh-Durham, Nortel published third-quarter results showing sales of fibre-optic gear had, for the first time in many quarters, failed to double year-over-year. Some investors sold shares, particularly those who based their holdings on momentum. Nortel's stock price began to weaken.

Roth held to his view that Nortel's revenue and operating profits in 2001 would grow between 30 per cent and 35 per cent – and he made it clear he expected the heads of his firm's business units to meet the targets. When investors continued driving down Nortel's share price, Roth responded by repeating his projection in press releases on Nov. 1, Nov. 20, Dec. 14 and Jan. 18. Roth could not accept that the tide had turned.

Shortly before the meeting in North Carolina, the heads of the business units learned, separately, that Qwest and other carriers were suddenly having trouble raising money. Nortel's top customers were now saying they would have to scale back orders.

The extent of the reversal was about to become clear to Nortel's top managers as a group. When the executives finally settled in position around the conference table, Frank Dunn – the company's chief financial officer – began seeking updates. He gestured to Mumford. For the first time in as long as anyone there could remember, the head of the optical products unit predicted a decline in sales prospects. Dunn paused, absorbing the bad news. Then he canvassed the other unit leaders – of wireless products, Internet telephony and enterprise technology. The outlook in every case was worse than expected.

For a moment, there was dead silence. Everyone realized an important line had been crossed. What they knew, what Dunn realized more than anyone, was that investors had to be told quickly about the dramatic change in Nortel's outlook.

Dunn reached Roth at the company's offices in France, where the CEO had been reviewing the firm's plans for wireless technologies. "To say I was shocked is an understatement," Roth later acknowledged, comparing the level of his astonishment to the one he experienced later that year when terrorists crashed aircraft into New York's twin towers. The CEO contacted board chairman Red Wilson and told him a press release was being developed.

At Nortel's suddenly sombre facility in Raleigh-Durham, Dunn turned to Tom Manley. "You're coming with me to Brampton," he told Chandran's top finance executive. Both men were rattled. They prided themselves on their ability to closely track business trends and felt they had been blindsided by the suddenness of the change in their customers' order books.

Some colleagues were less charitable – they said Nortel's most senior executives had seen what they wanted to see and had been unwilling to challenge Roth's sales targets for being unrealistic. At Brampton headquarters, Manley and Dunn worked into the night recalibrating Nortel's financial forecasts.

Roth delivered the unwelcome news to investors on Feb. 15, noting that Nortel's sales would grow just 15 per cent in 2001. This was half the growth he had projected just four weeks earlier. Yet even this downgrade would prove hopelessly optimistic. In coming months, Roth would have to make several more major changes to company guidance. By yearend, Nortel would eke out sales of little more than $17 billion, a moonshot short of the promised $40 billion.

"Our customers continued to search for new sources of funding to complete their networks and while they did so, reassured us that they would buy our equipment," Roth recalls, "but month by month they conceded that they could not secure financing and cancelled their orders."

Nortel was horribly exposed. The company had spent billions to build manufacturing facilities and open offices around the globe. It had also paid a fortune in signing bonuses to new employees and rewarded its executives with princely sums – more than $200 million in total compensation in 2000 for its top five executives alone – which was now seriously at odds with the coming era of austerity.

The company was also unexpectedly in the midst of a leadership crisis. For months Roth had stepped back from day-to-day management to give Chandran more freedom to put his stamp on Nortel. Chandran had been heir apparent since his appointment as chief operating officer the previous year, but the reality was he had faced no serious competition for the top job for much longer than that.

Chandran earned his privileged status in 1996 when Newbridge Networks Corp. – the telecommunications equipment firm founded by Kanata billionaire Terence Matthews – lured him to become CEO. Nortel's board of directors learned of Chandran's imminent defection just as Newbridge was set to announce it.

In fact, the press release had already been prepared. In order to convince Chandran to stay, Nortel's directors took the unusual step of promising him the inside track for the top job upon Roth's retirement, scheduled for the fall of 2001.

Roth was eager to retire. Visitors to his office in 2000 noticed he had already begun a countdown of the days to his exit. Then, early in 2001, he began to make plans to leave even earlier, perhaps in the spring. Two developments put an end to this. First was the phone call he received from Dunn after the Raleigh-Durham session. Second was the fact that Chandran – the executive who had done more than anyone to expand Nortel's physical presence, who had enthusiastically embraced the excesses of the telecom bubble economy – was nowhere to be seen.

Citing complications from a knife wound sustained when he had tried to defend himself from a robber on a late 1990s business trip to Singapore, Chandran bowed out. The wound was real but his closest colleagues knew that Chandran – an engaging salesman – was temperamentally unsuited to the job at hand.

That brutal task was left to Roth and Dunn, who became CEO in November 2001. Nortel started that year with 95,000 workers on the payroll. By yearend 2002, the company employed just 37,000.

Between them, Roth and Dunn closed 20 million square feet of real estate and cancelled thousands of contracts with suppliers. Nortel's accountants and lawyers prepared quick estimates for how long the offices would remain empty and how much the company would have to pay to settle lawsuits threatened by suppliers. Projections were made for severance pay and the value of medical and other fringe benefits that would be used by employees put on layoff notice.

Nortel's finance group tabulated these and other future liabilities and forklifted them onto the company's ledger. By mid-2002, Nortel's balance sheet was groaning with more than $5 billion in accrued liabilities, also known as accruals or reserves. These were costs that had been incurred but not yet paid. They were up sharply from the more usual average of $3.7 billion recorded during the last half of 2000. (It was normal for Nortel to maintain a fairly large balance of accruals to recognize obligations – such as software upgrades and next-generation technology – related to customer contracts.)

The danger with placing so many new reserves so quickly on the balance sheet became obvious later when Nortel realized it had overestimated what it required to cover contingencies. Lawsuits were settled for less than expected, the company found firms to sublet empty buildings, suppliers with a claim disappeared, customers declined promised upgrades of technology – the world did not end.

In the years to come, outside investigators and prosecutors would focus intensely on how Nortel's accountants added to and subtracted from its tower of reserves. They would also read much – far too much –

into why Nortel set up the liabilities and how the company justified removing them from the books.

In January 2005, independent lawyers hired by Nortel's audit committee concluded that Nortel's accounting for reserves did not comply with U.S. generally accepted accounting principles (GAAP), notably Statement of Financial Accounting Standards Number 5, which governs entries for contingencies. SFAS-5 sets out a couple of key conditions for booking an entry, namely that a future exposure, such as a lawsuit or an obligation to upgrade software, is both probable and capable of being estimated.

A company can remove a reserve from the balance sheet when the risks, or a portion of them, have been resolved. Decisions about how much to reserve and when to remove some or all of the liability are inherently complex, and require much judgment.

The independent lawyers – Wilmer Cutler Pickering Hale and Dorr of Washington, D.C. – alleged that Nortel's senior finance group "stretched the judgment … to create a flexible tool to achieve earnings-before-taxes targets," and "failed to correct the company's financial statements to account for the significant excess accrued liabilities."

These themes were echoed by Ontario Crown attorney Robert Hubbard. In 2012 he argued that criminal fraud had occurred, accusing Dunn, Beatty and Gollogly of deliberately exaggerating the size of these reserves, which he called cookie jars. Hubbard alleged that the accused reached into the jars at a convenient time to improperly remove liabilities. This action had the effect of boosting earnings, timed to trigger a variety of executive bonus programs then in place at Nortel.

Judge Marrocco reached a very difficult conclusion. He determined that Nortel had been accounting for its reserves within the rules – that the company had for many years used an accounting convention known as 'conservatism.' Put simply, this rule encourages the early recognition of unfavourable risks, especially in volatile industries.

Marrocco noted that Nortel lost billions in 2001 and 2002. "I do not find it unusual that sensible people confronted with that reality would think that the worst-case scenario was the best estimate of the risks to Nortel's assets." The judge added that the same people "would be slow to decrease accrued liabilities already on the balance sheet."

In 2001 Nortel's revenues dropped faster than costs. "The action we were taking was just not adequate," Roth said. "Each downsizing was not enough and the repeated layoffs were taking too long, draining cash and killing morale."

Nortel had to perform an excruciating balancing act. The deeper and swifter the downsizing, the more that had to be set aside to cover the associated restructuring costs. But there was an important benefit – making the company smaller would lower the annual costs of doing business in the years ahead.

So it proved. In 2000, Nortel recorded charges of $130 million related to eliminating 2,000 positions. The following year, the company set aside $1.4 billion to terminate 36,000 employees. The payoff: In 2002, Nortel spent less than $5 billion on engineering, administration and sales, compared to $9.1 billion the year before – an annual saving of $4 billion.

There were obvious limits to what Roth's finance managers could do under GAAP, which spelled out the rules for recording liabilities. Deloitte, the independent auditor, had dozens of employees on site all year, performing what was known as a continuous audit.

Nortel also employed a system of checks and balances. Controllers – the accountants who made the entries on the company's general ledger – operated independently of the heads of finance for each of the business units. This was to minimize the temptation for finance chiefs to bully accountants into making favourable entries.

Nortel also employed a group of internal auditors to scrutinize entries to make sure they conformed to ever-evolving accounting rules and a group of in-house lawyers who signed off on accounting entries that involved estimates of how much Nortel would pay to settle lawsuits, among other liabilities.

The message Roth sent in 2001 was simple: Don't kill the company's chances by being too cautious. "I wanted to remove any excuse for the business units to not act as quickly as possible," he said. "Survival of the company depended on bringing down the breakeven point as soon as possible."

Such was the impetus for one of the deepest and fastest downsizings in Canadian corporate history. And it looked like it might work. The only significant glitch had been in accounting. The restructuring had been done so quickly that paperwork on a number of recorded liabilities had gone missing. After scouring the June 30, 2003, balance sheet, the company found $952 million worth of liabilities – about seven per cent of the total – that lacked proper documentation and should have been removed in earlier periods. Nortel restated its results in the fall for the relevant periods. That seemed to be the end of it.

But within a matter of weeks the consequences of the fateful board decision to hire Wilmer Cutler came into view.

2

A Puzzling Encounter

Frank Dunn waited impatiently in his office for his last appointment of the day. Chief executive of Nortel Networks for the past two years, he had been instructed by his board of directors to take this meeting on his own – no lawyers, no advisers. Two Washington lawyers and a forensic accountant would ask him a few questions. That was all.

It was approaching 5 p.m., near dusk on this February day in 2004, and his visitors were almost two hours late. Dunn was feeling squeezed. He was to make sales calls the next day in Europe and the company plane, a Bombardier business jet, was leaving Toronto at dawn.

The CEO took in the view outside his second-floor office at the company's sprawling headquarters in Brampton. It had been a warm day, a few degrees above zero, and parts of the nearby ice-encrusted pond were obscured by haze. Dunn had turned 50 the previous month and his thinning hair was mostly white. The window reflected a gaze hardened by an ultra-competitive streak. A former jock, Dunn played tight end for McGill University's football squad in the early-1970s while earning his business degree. When he got really excited about something – which happened often – his colleagues involuntarily stepped back to avoid the spray of his words.

A few years earlier, the idea that Dunn would now be serving as the top gun at Nortel Networks would have struck many in the organization as improbable. Nortel's finance group, where Dunn devoted his career, was a distinctive minority within the firm, representing fewer than two of every hundred employees. The unit was made up of chartered accountants – the detailed numbers professionals who were qualified to make entries on Nortel's general ledger – and business experts such as Dunn, who viewed the world from a higher plane.

Among other things, he calculated the value of companies Nortel purchased, arranged corporate financing, and briefed the burgeoning group of independent analysts who wrote reports about the firm for investors.

The knock against Dunn was that he had never mastered telecommunications technology or detailed accounting. He made up for it with an approach to business that was utterly relentless.

When company chairman Red Wilson sought a new CEO to replace John Roth in 2001, he picked Dunn, the one senior executive familiar with all of Nortel's dozens of product lines. "The time for visionaries is over," Wilson said. The collapse of the telecommunications equipment industry that year demanded a different set of skills – someone with a thorough understanding of how Nortel was put together, an executive capable of restoring the corporation to profitability.

Dunn hadn't really wanted the job. He had been Roth's right-hand man for a tumultuous decade and had seen what the job entailed. Dunn had also absorbed some of the opprobrium that had been heaped upon Roth after the telecom crash and he wasn't comfortable with the limelight. But he eventually determined it was time to step up.

Dunn was as surprised as everyone else at how quickly the tide turned. He signed a $1-billion deal in the first week of 2004 to sell Internet gear to Verizon, one of America's largest phone companies. Later the same month, Dunn closed the books on Nortel's first annual profit since 1997. There were other bits of good news that preceded his meeting with the Washington lawyers. The Dominion Bond Rating Service had upgraded its view of Nortel's debt to stable from negative. And independent financial analysts were forecasting a second consecutive year of profits, one in which Nortel would grow revenues faster than its rivals.

Even more remarkable, given the utter misery of the past three years – the period that became known as the industry's nuclear winter – Nortel had recently reclaimed the title of Canada's most valuable corporation with a market capitalization of nearly $50 billion Cdn. It was a far, far cry from the $366-billion Cdn. market value reached during the telecom bubble of 2000, but the idea that Nortel might die on his watch no longer tormented Dunn. It's why he had no qualms about taking his next meeting.

§

Laura Wertheimer entered Dunn's office just as winter daylight was fading into dusk. She was accompanied by William McLucas – her fellow law partner at Wilmer Cutler – and Stephen Burlone, a principal at Huron Consulting and a forensic accountant. McLucas was the only one of the three professionals known even vaguely to the general public – he was a former director of investigations for the U.S. Securities and Exchange Commission, a role that for a time made him one of America's top white-collar crime fighters.

Surprisingly though, it was Wertheimer leading the investigation of Nortel's accounts. She had joined Wilmer Cutler just a few months earlier and this was her first assignment with her new firm. An experienced litigation lawyer in her late 40s, Wertheimer had spent most of her career with little-known Gardner & Shea where she quietly advised accountants and lawyers on rules of professional conduct.

She got right to the point, noting that her team had been examining Dunn's computer files and was puzzled by the relatively small number of emails. Was Dunn using some kind of software program to eliminate them? If the intent was to shock, it worked: This would not be an ordinary interview. It was odd in another way – no one took detailed notes. There was no tape recorder, no video. Nor did the lawyers show Dunn documents.

One hour into the session, Dunn appeared increasingly puzzled about its purpose. He had been told by Nortel's in-house counsel that Wertheimer's job was to assess the quality of the company's revised financial results.

Dunn believed the accounting for the $952-million restatement had been above board, and saw the Wilmer Cutler review as little more than fact-checking. But as the interview progressed, it seemed that Wertheimer had another agenda. She was focusing on transactions involving Nortel's liabilities and how these had influenced quarterly profits. And she really wasn't asking questions – she was making assertions.

Wertheimer brought up his accountants' use of balance sheet reserves in the fourth quarter of 2002. She said Nortel had improperly added a sufficient number of new liabilities to turn an unexpected quarterly profit into the loss that Dunn had earlier forecast. The reserves were booked properly, Dunn replied. "What you get each quarter is what you get," he said, adding that any accountant would know "you don't book to (meet) a forecast."

Wertheimer added there were groups of liabilities that Dunn's staff had left on the company's balance sheet improperly, the 'cookie jars' as these came to be called. For instance, there was a $25-million reserve for an executive bonus to be awarded at the discretion of the CEO. Nortel used these cookie jars to manipulate earnings, she asserted.

Wertheimer and her colleagues left shortly before 11 p.m. Dunn remained in his office for a few minutes trying to piece together where this stuff was coming from. As CEO he had certified, in writing, that the accounting was correct. But he had relied on representations from Deloitte and Michael Gollogly – Nortel's top accountant. Something, suddenly, was very wrong.

What Dunn didn't know was that he was already powerless to alter the course of Nortel's tragic trajectory.

3

A Hard-Wired Investigation

The road to destruction started innocently enough, with a conversation in the fall of 2003 between Nortel's in-house counsel Nick DeRoma and David Becker, a partner in the Washington office of Cleary Gottlieb Steen & Hamilton. The lawyers had reason to chat frequently. Nortel relied on Cleary Gottlieb for advice about its operations in the U.S., which accounted for the largest single piece of Nortel's revenues.

After Nortel filed its restatement, DeRoma pondered whether the SEC was likely to follow up with an investigation. Becker had served as general counsel for the SEC until 2002, and was in good position to offer an opinion. At the time, the SEC was on the warpath against white-collar crime and Becker believed the SEC's interest in a Nortel probe would be high.

He and DeRoma agreed that having outside counsel give a second opinion on Nortel's books was less risky than waiting for the SEC to invite itself in. They suggested to the board that if Nortel voluntarily hired credible independent investigators to re-examine the company's financial statements, the SEC might forgo a probe of its own. Becker knew William McLucas – who had also worked at the SEC and was now a partner with Wilmer Cutler.

Late in October 2003, Nortel's top two directors – Red Wilson and John Cleghorn – made their way to the business aviation terminal at Toronto Pearson International Airport. The men were long-serving members of Canada's business establishment.

Wilson, a former CEO of Redpath Industries and Bell Canada Enterprises, had joined Nortel's board in 1991, when the telecommunications equipment maker had been majority owned by BCE. He was now Nortel's chairman. Cleghorn was a recent addition to Nortel's board – he became part of the club in 2001 after a long career at the Royal Bank of Canada, where he had served as CEO for seven years.

Cleghorn was head of Nortel's audit committee, which was responsible for overseeing the quality of the company's financial statements.

It was a Sunday morning, unusual for a business meeting. The directors greeted Wertheimer and McLucas. Becker and DeRoma rounded out the gathering. After some preliminaries, the group got down to business. They agreed that Wilmer Cutler would conduct a forensic audit of Nortel's June 30, 2003, balance sheet and the circumstances that had created the need for the $952-million restatement.

Wilson liked the idea of avoiding the SEC for another reason. The chairman believed such a probe would be too distracting for Nortel managers at a critical time in the company's turnaround. When Wilson said farewell that morning, McLucas reassured him, "This looks pretty straightforward."

What no one foresaw was the zeal with which Wertheimer and Burlone, the forensic accountant from Huron, would pursue their new assignment, and what early conclusions they would draw from such circumstantial evidence.

The investigators' powers were considerable. DeRoma warned employees that anyone who refused to meet them would be sacked. He added that Wilmer Cutler would have complete access to computer hard drives, emails and paper files, and instructed financial managers to organize the paperwork in their offices. The investigators would photocopy everything.

Douglas Beatty and Michael Gollogly at first weren't unduly alarmed by the invasiveness of the coming probe – the restatement had been large in absolute terms, even if it amounted to a small percentage of Nortel's total liabilities. The executives also knew that the company's return to profits in 2003 had been helped by a number of legitimate but unusual accounting transactions unrelated to operations, ones that required significant judgment. A second look could certainly be justified, they agreed.

They were also confident they could back up all their decisions. Indeed, Gollogly and his team felt they had pulled off a near miracle in fixing the errors on Nortel's balance sheet in time for the publication of the third-quarter results the previous fall.

Beatty met with Wertheimer and McLucas shortly after they landed their assignment and took them through the history of the accounting. He explained that in the second quarter of 2003 Nortel had discovered liabilities on its balance sheet that lacked proper paperwork. This had prompted a more comprehensive review which produced the revelation that the liabilities on Nortel's June balance sheet were overstated by $952 million.

The CFO described how his finance team and Gollogly's accountants had spent months identifying which liabilities should have been removed from the June balance sheet – and when. Some of the revisions went back several quarters. The main effect of the changes was to slightly reduce the very large net losses originally reported by Nortel in 2002 and 2001.

Wertheimer took notes and asked many questions. Her demeanour, and that of McLucas, was attentive, neutral. Beatty was at ease. It would be the last time he felt this way.

Despite Red Wilson's desire to avoid an SEC investigation, the U.S. agency still wanted a word. That was how Beatty found himself early in December at SEC headquarters in Washington, confronted by seven rather hostile commission employees. During a two-and-a-half-hour long session, Beatty offered his explanations for the restatement but was continually interrupted and challenged. The SEC officials seemed particularly suspicious about Nortel's use of balance sheet items that influenced quarterly earnings. All were taking copious notes.

Unbeknownst to Beatty, the SEC had been investigating the accounting of Nortel's archrival Lucent Technologies – and would charge that firm in May with accounting fraud in connection with how it recognized revenues upfront when these should have been reported in future periods. (Lucent would settle with the commission by paying a small fine but neither "admitted nor denied" the allegations.) The issues were similar but the facts differed from those underlying Nortel's restatement. However, the SEC appeared to be smelling blood when it came to telecom equipment-makers and how they dealt with the crash of their industry.

Beatty got little comfort from his legal team. Three in-house lawyers, led by DeRoma, accompanied him to the SEC grilling, along with a handful of others from Cleary Gottlieb, who offered perspective on U.S. issues. The lawyers interjected a few times during the session. But for the most part, Beatty was alone in offering a defence. It was a sign of things to come.

§

Wilmer Cutler and Huron Consulting ramped up the investigation in December by dispatching a small army of associates and investigators to Nortel's Brampton headquarters. They would attach themselves to their Nortel host for more than two years and their billings would eventually reach tens of millions of dollars. The U.S. specialists grabbed offices and desks recently vacated by sacked Nortel employees, and then turned their attention to downloading and organizing hundreds of thousands of business records and emails. They mixed uneasily with the Nortel staff who watched nervously as the interlopers grabbed their colleagues' files and rifled through them for evidence. Of what, the Nortel employees couldn't be sure.

Wertheimer began her interviews on Jan. 7, starting with Beatty. She was joined by McLucas and accountants from Huron. "It was completely adversarial," Beatty told a colleague at the time, expressing his surprise at the change in tone from the introductory session he had had with them just a few weeks earlier.

Beginning with the query she would later pose to Dunn, Wertheimer demanded to know where Beatty kept the rest of his emails, the ones he didn't keep on his computer hard drive. She questioned the CFO about why Nortel had released (removed) $80 million worth of first-quarter liabilities that lacked proper paperwork, even though the changes had been disclosed in a press release and approved by Nortel's external auditors, Deloitte.

Eight years later, Beatty would watch with satisfaction as Judge Marrocco received evidence showing how the accounting for the $80 million had not only been proper, it had not been responsible for triggering the executive bonus plan as alleged by the Crown. But on this day, however, Beatty's explanations on this and other accounting items couldn't find purchase – the investigators already seemed to be heading down a certain track.

The direction became somewhat clearer during Wertheimer's interviews with Michael Gollogly, the keeper of Nortel's general ledger. Beginning on Jan. 9, Wertheimer and Burlone handed Gollogly binders that summarized how Nortel's accountants had justified various large entries. The most important of these items would become known as the Wilmer Cutler 14. These were complex transactions involving, among other things, the accounting for Genuity – a bankrupt Nortel customer – and fringe benefits for Nortel's U.S. employees. Details for these items would accumulate gradually in the months and years to come.

The investigators facing Gollogly touched again on the $80-million transaction in the first quarter of 2003. They also referred to the 303, one of several alleged cookie jars used to manipulate earnings. Gollogly and Beatty insisted the unsupported liabilities reflected nothing more sinister than the out-of-control downsizing Nortel had experienced. Wertheimer appeared skeptical.

There was one other item on the agenda: Wertheimer wanted to know why Gollogly had approved a number of late entries involving the fourth quarter of 2002. These had created a loss from what looked to be a profit.

This baffled Gollogly. He had expected questions on the first two quarters of 2003, when Nortel had declared its first profits in years. "Why are they going on now about the fourth quarter?" he asked Deloitte auditor Don Hathway at the time. Gollogly's third and final interview with Wilmer Cutler took place on Jan. 21, two weeks after Wertheimer had launched her interrogations. At that point, the Washington lawyer and her colleagues had interviewed just three people – Beatty, Gollogly and Karen Sledge, Nortel's controller in the U.S.

Yet the basic thrust of their investigation already seemed hard-wired, indeed would scarcely change in the years to come, through to the criminal trial of 2012. Cookie jars, secretive earnings forecasts, balance sheet manipulations, executive bonuses: these were the common themes that suited the temper of the times.

4

Through the Prism of Enron

January 2004 was not a good month for either Beatty or Gollogly, quite aside from the interviews they endured at the hands of Wilmer Cutler. Although Beatty had taken some holidays over Christmas, he was still fighting exhaustion. He had spent much of the previous year doing double-duty. As CFO, he was trying to ensure the corporation had enough cash and flexibility in its financial structure to survive.

He had also been pressed into service to meet with key customers around the globe to reassure them that Nortel would be around for years to come and that it should be retained as a key supplier of telecommunications gear and services. He did an especially draining series of visits to European centres before Christmas. It took Beatty a couple of weeks after his break to get back into his normal routine. Later, Wilmer Cutler queried why there were so few entries in

Beatty's personal journal during this period. "What's he leaving out?" one investigator asked Beatty's assistant.

Gollogly was facing a different set of pressures, not least of which was heightened interest from just about everybody on the state of Nortel's balance sheet. Nortel's external auditor, Deloitte, had asked him to conduct a quick review of the Dec. 31 balance sheet – basically an update of the June 30 snapshot that had been the focus of the restatement. It was an unusual request, though, because it came several weeks earlier than was considered normal, and Deloitte wanted it done quickly. Deloitte had signed off on Nortel's original books and the restatement and it wanted no more surprises.

There was nothing particularly difficult about a review of the items on the balance sheet. The issue was time. Nortel's liabilities comprised hundreds of thousands of entries. Gollogly persuaded Deloitte it was impossible to do a full review with the staff on hand at the speed demanded. So they compromised. Gollogly's team sampled the most significant balance sheet items, representing the vast majority of Nortel's liabilities by value. The Dec. 31 review proved satisfactory to Deloitte. Even so, Gollogly ordered his staff to continue scrutiny of the full balance sheet. Given enough time, he believed, he would eliminate all items that currently lacked paperwork.

Then in mid-February, a shocker. Wertheimer and Burlone called to lower the threshold for a full balance sheet review from $100,000 per item to zero. Gollogly took the call in his office with Sledge. They stared at each other in disbelief. Wilmer Cutler wanted to account for every penny on the corporation's $12-billion balance sheet of liabilities. The investigators were insisting they achieve the impossible. It was also a mathematical near-certainty that the revised threshold – it would eventually drop to $10,000 per balance sheet entry – would produce different totals.

That wasn't all. Wilmer Cutler also tightened its scrutiny of the movements of liabilities in 2002 and 2003. The manner in which these items were added to or removed from the balance sheet could heavily influence earnings. During the 2003 restatement, Gollogly's group had examined the setup and release of every accrual valued at more than $2 million – a threshold that had originally been established by Deloitte. Wilmer Cutler eventually pushed this down to $100,000.

Frank Dunn was unaware of the extra demands on Gollogly. The CEO had been warned by counsel not to discuss his dealings with the U.S. investigators so he hadn't asked Gollogly about his interviews. Nor could Dunn demand answers from Nortel's independent auditors at Deloitte. But after his own session with Wertheimer and Burlone, Dunn was very concerned about where the investigation was going.

Before he left the next day for Europe, he instructed Beatty to take a second look at the accounting. He also asked Jim Goodfellow, an experienced Deloitte auditor on the Nortel account, to help out. They discovered that Gollogly was already trying to satisfy the investigators that Nortel's accounting had met the appropriate standards.

Gollogly, Beatty and Goodfellow assigned more staff to analyze the accounting related to the movement of liabilities – including the 14 large accruals that were of particular interest to Wilmer Cutler. They made hundreds of calls in February and March to Nortel colleagues to confirm why liabilities had been established and whether there were still reasons to keep them on the books. Gollogly applied his microscope to Nortel's balance sheet.

As they raced to fill in the gaps of their knowledge, they didn't know they were nearly out of time.

Just 16 days after she met with Dunn, Wertheimer would privately advise a senior Deloitte lawyer of her concerns about accounting practices at Nortel, adding it was likely that a second restatement would be required.

Nine days after that, on March 15, Wertheimer's early conclusions would prompt Nortel chairman Red Wilson to put his company's CFO and controller on leave. Before April was out, Dunn, Beatty and Gollogly were sacked 'for cause' and would become the target for multiple civil and criminal investigations.

It would take nearly a decade before the outside world learned just how little hard evidence had informed the board's precipitous action. When Judge Marrocco dismissed all charges against Dunn, Beatty and Gollogly in 2013, it was after a yearlong trial that had reviewed a library of evidence.

Among the hundreds of documents introduced at trial were PowerPoint presentations and emails suggesting that during its probe Wilmer Cutler was aware that Deloitte had closely examined, and signed off on, the accounting transactions considered problematic, including the Wilmer Cutler 14. A key document, dated Jan. 20, 2003, was a progress report on Deloitte's yearend audit. It covered dozens of accounting issues ranging from Nortel's forecasting process to how the company was recording reserves for items contained in the Wilmer Cutler 14.

Still other exhibits suggested that the accounting Wilmer Cutler substituted for Nortel's original numbers in a second restatement reflected different interpretations of legitimate accounting rules, or incorporated new guidelines that had been applied retroactively. Some of the differences had nothing to do with Nortel's accountants – they were grounded in disputes between Deloitte's U.S. and Canadian auditors.

As for the $303-million cookie jar? The court would learn most of it had not existed – and that what little remained had been dealt with properly.

There had been no fraud.

Around the time Marrocco rendered his decision, Wilmer Cutler (now WilmerHale) revised Wertheimer's biography on the company website. Gone was the earlier reference to Wertheimer "serving as co-lead counsel in (the) audit committee investigation for Nortel Networks involving multibillion-dollar issues relating to revenue recognition and reserve manipulation." This section was replaced by a more generic description of her duties. Wertheimer's lengthy stint at Nortel was no longer worthy of mention.

§

There are many reasons why Nortel failed as a corporation, but the events that occurred in the 100 plus days between the first interviews conducted by Wertheimer and the firing of Nortel's most powerful financial executives were pivotal. By accepting Wilmer Cutler's quick assessment of the firm's accounting at face value, Nortel's board of directors left the corporation fatally vulnerable to the recession of 2008 and 2009.

The onset of a host of investigations into Nortel's books contributed greatly. Nortel, which based its decision on Wilmer Cutler's conclusions, settled quickly with the U.S. Securities and Exchange Commission and the Ontario Securities Commission, and co-operated with the RCMP and the Attorney General in Texas.

Nortel paid token fines of $1 million to the OSC and $35 million to the SEC. The criminal and civil cases against the company were dropped, leaving Dunn, Beatty and Gollogly as the remaining targets.

Disgruntled shareholders were a bigger problem for Nortel. They eventually settled for $575 million in cash, sapping the company's financial strength. The distractions caused by multiple restatements over the next three years weakened the firm further. Mike Zafirovski, the CEO from 2005 to 2009, estimated the company spent $400 million on outside accounting professionals and employee salaries in the effort to get the numbers to where Wilmer Cutler thought they should be.

So eager were Nortel's new CEOs – Bill Owens until 2005, then Zafirovski – to demonstrate the corporation was under ethical new management they swept out most of the senior management group, depriving Nortel of some of its most knowledgeable talent. This happened when Nortel should have been preparing to take on lower-cost rivals from China by remaking its technologies. Instead, it was constantly on the defensive, seeking to sell one business unit and then another in the hunt for cash and synergies – and finding neither.

The stigma associated with the allegedly dirty accounting hurt in other ways as well. Late in 2008, when Zafirovski sought $1 billion in aid from the federal government to avoid slipping into bankruptcy protection, he was turned down. In part, it was because the Conservatives believed Nortel hadn't played by the rules, and had brought this on itself.

The government was right about the latter assertion, but not in the way it believed then. Nortel's directors – the stewards of a century-old enterprise that had survived multiple wars and a Great Depression – had buckled in the face of pressure from Wilmer Cutler. The board had put Nortel's CFO and controller on leave in part because the investigators had warned that unless the company took action quickly, the SEC would likely come down hard.

Of course the directors had reason to take Wilmer Cutler and its senior partner William McLucas seriously. Quite aside from his previous job as director of investigations for the SEC, McLucas had recently played a role cleaning up high-profile accounting scandals in the U.S. He helped the boards of directors for Enron and Worldcom analyze what had gone wrong and implement policies to prevent similar misdeeds. In the case of Enron, Wilmer Cutler assigned more than 30 lawyers who completed their report in 90 days.

Enron, an energy services giant, had hidden billions of dollars' worth of liabilities from investors by storing them in illegal entities away from the balance sheet. Worldcom, a customer of Nortel, had used fraudulent accounting to mask a dramatic decline in company earnings. Top executives from Enron and Worldcom were jailed for their transgressions, and the U.S. Congress in 2002 passed the Sarbanes-Oxley Act, which compels senior executives of public corporations to certify their accounting is accurate.

The charges at Enron and Worldcom created a certain kind of prism through which Wertheimer, McLucas and Burlone viewed Nortel's numbers. Another influence was the SEC's drive in the late 1990s to crack down on a number of accounting practices that public firms were using to manage their earnings. These were enumerated in a landmark speech on Sept. 28, 1998, by SEC chairman Arthur Levitt, and included such things as "big bath" restructuring charges, premature recognition of revenues and cookie jar reserves.

Big bath restructuring and cookie jar reserves referred to the practice of overestimating costs and liabilities up front in order to create a financial cushion in future, when earnings might be lower than forecast.

For instance, three months after Levitt's speech, the SEC charged W.R. Grace, a chemical conglomerate, with having improved earnings from 1993 to 1995 by releasing some contents from its cookie jar.

The latter had been created, the SEC alleged, when the company stockpiled higher-than-expected revenues in 1991 and 1992 rather than attributing them to the quarters in which they were actually received. In 1999, W.R. Grace agreed to a cease and desist order "without admitting or denying the SEC's findings." The company's civil penalty: It established a $1-million fund to further general awareness of generally accepted accounting principles.

A case that resonated more strongly with Nortel executives was that of Microsoft, the software giant that agreed in June 2002 to cease and desist from certain accounting violations. Among the SEC's allegations was that Microsoft had materially misstated its earnings between 1994 and 1998 because it had failed to properly substantiate the accounting for reserves allocated for obsolete inventories, excess manufacturing facilities and the like. The SEC chided Microsoft for its lack of safeguards for ensuring that adjustments to these reserve accounts were done in compliance with U.S. GAAP. Microsoft settled with the SEC under an administrative order "without admitting or denying the findings."

A senior member of Nortel's finance group at the time recalls, "We all thought the Microsoft settlement was pretty significant."

The SEC was signalling its intention to examine very closely companies' accounting for reserves, to make sure existing rules were being followed. That is what Nortel's senior finance executives believed they had been doing. But Wilmer Cutler viewed with suspicion the removal of liabilities that bumped up Nortel's earnings.

The board wasn't alone in failing to challenge Wilmer Cutler's early conclusions. Deloitte had been immersed in Nortel's accounting for a century and had given the audit committee its assurance the numbers met all its tests.

Deloitte partner Don Hathway was aware of the work being undertaken by his fellow auditors to establish proper support for the items on Nortel's balance sheet. Yet, neither Hathway nor his colleague John Cawthorne persuaded Wertheimer that explanations other than earnings manipulation might have been at play.

Deloitte later excused its failure to push back by noting that in a forensic audit – unlike a conventional one – investigators have access to emails and other material from computer hard drives. If allegedly suspicious emails had been ripped from context, as the 2012 trial would show, that wasn't Deloitte's fault, the accounting giant maintained. Deloitte was determined not to take the fall for whatever Nortel's financial executives might or might not have done.

Ordinary Canadians were even faster to judge Nortel. In the weeks following his firing, Dunn discovered his new status in a most personal way. Some friends remained loyal but others stopped calling. When he and his wife visited a local restaurant in Oakville, the other diners suddenly stopped talking. No one came to say hello. Dunn quit his role as adviser to QCL Growth Partners of Ottawa in 2007, after news of his assignment was made public. The proprietor received so many angry calls and emails Dunn decided it wasn't worth it. In a pro shop, he overheard people talking with his golf partners. "Why do you people even talk to him?" they were saying.

Things got worse after criminal charges were laid in 2008. Ian Craig, former chief marketing officer at Nortel and a longtime friend of Dunn, noticed the change during a golf match shortly after that. "He was as listless as I've ever seen him," Craig said.

But there was little general sympathy for Nortel's senior executives. Not only had they failed to anticipate their industry's dramatic slide, they had extracted tens of millions of dollars in pay, bonuses and stock options before the company's fall.

When Wilmer Cutler unearthed what it said was evidence of improper accounting, the public was all too willing to believe the worst. The surprise is that so, too, had the company's directors.

§

On a clear, cool evening late in February 2004, a black Town Car pulled up to the front entrance of the Toronto Club in the heart of the city's financial district. The three-storey sandstone edifice is home to the country's oldest private club, open to new members by invitation only. Nortel chairman Red Wilson and CEO Frank Dunn, buried deep in conversation, seemed not to notice their surroundings as they entered the 115-year-old building.

Inside, they were to meet a handful of other directors following a regular company board meeting. As was usually the case when Wilmer Cutler gave a presentation, Dunn hadn't been invited to the directors' session. Now he was learning that the Washington lawyers had had some unsettling things to say about Nortel's accounting. "The first indications that there might have been some difficulties with the firm's reporting came to light," Wilson said later, adding these were "not conclusive as to reasons."

There had been talk of the 303 cookie jar and some discussion about the company's accounting for reserves, especially during the first two quarters of 2003 when transactions unrelated to operations had helped to produce profits. A second restatement loomed. The directors hadn't liked the implications. Even if no fraud were involved, and it was a matter of cleaning up accounting errors, another restatement would be deeply embarrassing and could cut short the firm's apparent recovery.

Nortel's directors spent part of their dinner debating whether to sack Gollogly and Beatty right away. One board member suggested installing Kate Stevenson, Nortel's treasurer, as CFO. Dunn, clearly becoming alarmed, asked to see Wilmer Cutler's evidence. Wilson urged him not to worry, adding that the board would take its time.

The idea that Wertheimer may have been simply applying different accounting judgments was given short shrift, and ongoing work by Beatty, Gollogly and Deloitte's auditors to double-check the items of concern to Wilmer Cutler was ignored. Most surprising of all, no one was asking why Deloitte – which had given a favourable opinion of the original restatement – wasn't giving a defence of its earlier work on the Nortel file. A conclusion that errors had occurred, let alone deliberate wrongdoing, seemed premature.

Dunn was also annoyed by the evening's tenor for an entirely personal reason. Wilson had billed the dinner as a celebration of Dunn's success in saving the company. The directors presented him with a framed line drawing. In it, Captain Dunn was on the deck of a ship, completely surrounded by the company's smiling directors.

5

'I've Been Suspended?'

Bruce Richmond, the Deloitte partner in charge of managing the Nortel relationship, knew a problem when he saw it. Nine days after the directors' Toronto Club dinner, the 36-year veteran of the accounting and auditing giant learned his company would almost certainly have to audit Nortel's 2002 and 2003 financial statements – again.

Deloitte had been Nortel's external auditor since before the First World War, which meant it had provided oversight for the firm's financial statements throughout its rise to a global telecom power, and through multiple restructurings as Nortel shifted unevenly from one product cycle to another. But Deloitte had never been through anything like the last few years.

Such was the scale of Nortel's downsizing in 2002, Richmond said, "groups of finance employees disappeared virtually overnight." Deloitte's auditors often worked late into the evening trying to make sure

Nortel's accounting lined up properly with all the restructuring. Deloitte had signed off on Nortel's $952-million restatement.

But now Wilmer Cutler had determined that that restatement was incomplete and said it would recommend to Nortel's directors that another one be done. This did not look good on Deloitte, never mind Nortel. On the first Saturday in March, one of Deloitte's U.S. lawyers called Wertheimer for a private briefing. She "brought information to our firm that had previously not been known," Richmond testified in 2012. Precisely what information he did not make clear, but it's likely she expanded on allegations of earnings manipulation.

The session worried Deloitte profoundly. Its own auditors, Cawthorne and Hathway, had signed off on items that Wilmer Cutler was now suggesting had been done improperly. Was Deloitte somehow exposed?

Just two years earlier, Arthur Andersen LLP had surrendered its licences to practise as a certified general accountant after being found guilty of criminal charges related to its handling of audits at Enron, a major client. Arthur Andersen had been one of the accounting industry's five biggest outfits, with a nearly 90-year track record, more than 80,000 employees and $9.3 billion in annual revenues. Although the U.S. Supreme Court later overturned the guilty verdict, it was too late. The damage to Arthur Andersen's reputation was complete and its various global entities had either been closed or acquired by competitors.

Deloitte was keen to avoid a similar fate. On March 7, the day after Wertheimer briefed Deloitte's lawyer, Richmond conferred with Nortel's two top directors, Wilson and Cleghorn. The details of that meeting weren't made public, but shortly after Nortel instructed Wilmer Cutler to stay away from Deloitte's working files. Cleghorn testified that had he given Wilmer Cutler free rein, Deloitte may have decided to "leave the premises" – and Nortel, he said, could not afford to have its auditor leave at such a critical time.

The declaration that Deloitte's working papers were off-limits meant Wilmer Cutler would conduct the rest of its investigation without crucial pieces of intelligence. One such Deloitte memo had analyzed in detail the accounting related to $80 million worth of items in the first quarter of 2003 – a matter of special focus for Wilmer Cutler. The memo showed how the accounting had been done according to U.S. GAAP and said that the payment of bonuses had also been appropriate.

Despite their lack of access to certain Deloitte papers, Wertheimer and her colleagues were not operating in the dark. Nortel's managers forwarded many key Deloitte documents, including hundreds that involved email exchanges between Deloitte and Nortel employees. The emails showed there had been extensive dialogue between the two groups over issues that concerned Wilmer Cutler.

Yet the independent investigators seemed unimpressed.

§

Wilmer Cutler's views would be given a full airing at a critical March 10 board meeting at company headquarters in Brampton. Sadly, the nine non-management directors of Nortel were not, as a group, well-suited for the task at hand.

Many had done well in business, law and politics. But, with the exception of Red Wilson, the former chief executive of BCE, none had significant experience in the telecommunications equipment industry. James Blanchard, the former U.S. ambassador to Canada, and Yves Fortier, a partner with Ogilvy Renault, were lawyers. Other directors had a background in business: Robert Ingram was a senior executive with pharmaceutical giant GlaxoSmithKline of Britain; Robert Brown was CEO of Bombardier as well as a former senior federal civil servant; Bill Owens, a director since 2002, had been a senior executive with SAIC.

One of Nortel's biggest rivals, Cisco Systems of California, employed a much different formula: Nearly all its directors were familiar with the terrain on which their company fought. In 2004, eight of Cisco's 12 directors were current or former senior executives at high-tech firms. Two were former deans of engineering at Stanford University and two others were former audit partners with KPMG and Arthur Andersen. There was one other distinctive difference – Cisco's former CEO, John Morgridge, was also on the board.

A former boss can offer an important reality check on the plans of the current chief executive, as well as perspective and institutional history. However, following the departure of Paul Stern as CEO in 1992, Nortel's directors passed a policy to prohibit former chief executives from remaining on the board.

The impact of this move was incalculable. Had either of Stern's successors as CEO – Jean Monty or John Roth – been part of the board that listened to Wilmer Cutler's first few presentations, there is little doubt they would have insisted on seeing more hard evidence of transgressions or error before putting Nortel's controller and CFO on paid leave.

Until he retired in the fall of 2001, Roth, a radio engineer and lifetime employee, effectively controlled the company's board in collaboration with Wilson. Roth had a profound grasp of telecommunications technology and could explain it in terms anyone could understand. It helped that Nortel's share price sextupled during his tenure as CEO, reaching a split-adjusted peak of $1,231 on the Toronto Stock Exchange on July 26, 2000. Roth made believers of the directors, many of whom had made a small fortune on Nortel share options.

When Frank Dunn took over as CEO, he held no similar sway over the directors. The board was overwhelmingly dominated by Wilson – the longest-serving director – and Cleghorn.

Cleghorn at least possessed some relevant background – he was a chartered accountant – but he does not appear to have second-guessed Wilmer Cutler's early conclusions about Nortel's accounting. Certainly he had plenty of opportunity to make his views known since he had hired the outside investigators and oversaw their work. Accordingly, he met more frequently with Wertheimer than any of Nortel's other directors and was familiar with how Wilmer Cutler's thinking progressed.

When Wertheimer and McLucas conducted their day-long presentation to the board in Brampton on March 10, they had a unique advantage in making their case. There was no former CEO, the directors as a group were not formidable experts in accounting and Cleghorn – the man who hired them – seemed determined to stay neutral. Even the auditors were new to the file.

By sheer happenstance, Deloitte picked late 2002 to begin rotating its top two auditors on the Nortel file. Out went Richard Clarke as the most senior Canadian auditor, in came John Cawthorne. Early in 2003, Mitch Szorcsik was replaced by Don Hathway as the senior U.S. audit partner for the Nortel account. Clarke and Szorcsik had given favourable opinions of Nortel's accounting through to the day each left.

The Wilmer Cutler team summarized the key accounting transactions and gave Nortel's directors their reasons for the need to revise Nortel's financial statements a second time.

Many of the accounting items were complex deals involving Nortel customers such as Genuity and PWC, and Nortel products such as Optical DX. None of it was easy to absorb, especially for directors who lacked expertise in contract accounting. For instance, the PWC accrual emerged from a 2002 decision by Nortel to bring back in-house a number of jobs it had outsourced to PWC two years earlier.

Because the move provoked a number of disputes over invoices, Nortel set up a provision on its balance sheet equivalent to its estimated exposure in a lawsuit. The company eliminated the provision in the first quarter of 2003 when the two parties formally resolved their differences, and the release of the provision had the effect of increasing profits that quarter.

But Wilmer Cutler questioned whether Nortel should have established the provision in the first place, and also queried the timing for its eventual release. Debate turned on whether Nortel and PWC had settled their differences in the fourth quarter of 2002 or the first quarter of 2003. The trial in 2012 considered the evidence.

After Dunn and his colleagues were fired, Wilmer Cutler sought an outside legal opinion, which held that the formal disengagement agreement was "substantially complete" by Dec. 13, 2002.

However, the same evidence showed that a deal had not been reached with PWC in France, nor would it be until Jan. 17. In short, the new opinion was no more reasonable than the original one.

The accounting involving another of Nortel's customers – Genuity Inc., a Boston-based Internet services provider – gives an even better insight into the difficult issues that emerged. Nortel recorded a $19-million accrual during the telecom boom to recognize a longer-term obligation to help Genuity develop and market its optical products. It also set up a $19-million reserve to support Black Rocket, a next-generation network, being promoted by Genuity.

But in 2002 Genuity went bankrupt and its assets were acquired by Level 3 Communications, another Nortel customer. This, in turn, prompted Nortel to question whether its obligation to Genuity still existed. An outside law firm, Lovells, advised that it did not – meaning Nortel no longer had to make good its $19-million commitment to finance Genuity's dreams.

At the same time, Nortel reduced the Black Rocket provision by $4 million. The result: Nortel reduced its original $38-million Genuity accrual to just $15 million, thus improving earnings in the first quarter of 2003.

During its probe, Wilmer Cutler conducted an exhaustive examination of the $23-million release. Trial exhibits showed there were 13 meetings involving eight Nortel accounting staff and six Deloitte auditors. In mid-May 2004, a 21-page analysis examined the accounting options and settled on the one supported by Lovells.

This assessment was deemed 'final' on June 14, 2004, but was overruled by Deloitte's U.S. headquarters in Wilton, Conn. The U.S. group viewed the $23-million release as an error because, in its view, it should have occurred in the second quarter, not the first. The reason had to do with its interpretation of paperwork related to the Level 3 acquisition and when "derecognition of a liability" was permitted.

"It was an error that is understandable once the facts are known," Marrocco concluded in his ruling.

A third item in the Wilmer Cutler 14 involved a $5-million reserve established to recognize Nortel's potential liability to customers seeking a technology upgrade. The product in question was a piece of optical gear known as DX-3. Nortel's accountants set up the reserve in 2000 and 2001 when the company's engineers failed to deliver the DX-3 on time. Instead, the company shipped customers the then-current technology, the DX-1, with a promise to upgrade later. However, when the market for optical products collapsed, many Nortel customers declined delivery of the DX-3. Nortel reduced its reserve accordingly during the relevant quarters in late 2002 and early 2003, thus increasing earnings by a like amount.

Evidence produced at trial showed that Deloitte had signed off on the accounting, including the reasons for establishing the setup and initiating the releases. Later, after Wilmer Cutler got involved, Deloitte changed its interpretation of the applicable accounting rule. The auditor ruled the provision should not have been established in the first place, that Nortel should have deferred the revenue associated with the sale of the DX-3. Again, a difference of opinion over accounting.

In other words, Wilmer Cutler appeared to have nothing definitive. What they offered the directors were opinions. The investigators questioned the appropriateness of the accounting of significant entries, and re-examined the use of the 303 cookie jar. Further, they warned Nortel's directors the SEC would evaluate them based on how quickly they responded to knowledge of suspect accounting, whatever the cause.

§

Gollogly and Beatty had been waiting nearby in one of Nortel's smaller boardrooms.

They'd been kept on call for more than five hours – and would have substantially less time than Wilmer Cutler to make their own presentation. They, too, were relatively new faces as far as the board was concerned.

Gollogly, a native of Northern Ireland, joined Nortel in 1996 as a chartered accountant, serving as assistant controller. Somewhat gruff but self-assured, he spent the next several years in various assignments in Britain, Asia and France, where he was chief financial officer of the company's global wireless products unit. Gollogly was promoted to controller on July 25, 2002 – which made him head of accounting just as Nortel began trying to deal with its mountain of liabilities.

Like Gollogly, Beatty was a chartered accountant and had landed his assignment in July 2002 as well. Beatty joined Nortel's finance group in 1985 but left a decade later to become vice-president of finance for Sprint Canada. In 1999, just as the telecom equipment boom was close to its peak, Dunn enticed him back to Nortel with the controller's job. After Dunn was promoted to chief executive, Beatty became CFO.

Gollogly guided Nortel's directors through his team's analysis of the various accounting issues. He pointed out that he was completing his investigation of all the original setups and releases of accrued liabilities valued at $2 million plus each – and this included the 14 that really concerned Wilmer Cutler. Gollogly added that the documentation for those items was already in the hands of Deloitte. This aspect of the accounting had been accurate, he said.

Then Gollogly moved into new territory. He said his ongoing analysis of liabilities was showing that the 2003 restatement hadn't quite captured all of Nortel's excess reserves. In Australia, Europe and a couple of other entities within Nortel's sprawling global domain, managers had failed to identify and deal with some of these items.

Gollogly told the directors that he had uncovered some $300 million worth of new errors – items that sat on Nortel's balance sheet without supporting paperwork. Set against Nortel's total liabilities at the time of $12 billion, it wasn't the end of the world. But the timing was awful.

"Do we have a problem, here?" Wilson demanded. Gollogly replied that it was likely Nortel would miss its statutory deadline for filing its 2003 results. He did not have to add that a second restatement would likely be necessary, albeit one that had nothing to do with allegations of earnings manipulation.

Nortel's accountants and auditors were still dealing with the consequences of the firm's extraordinary downsizing. No one was happy with the way things were turning out.

§

Wilson felt he had no choice but to act. While Wilmer Cutler hadn't proved fraud, the investigators were going down that road. Nor were the accounts where they should have been. Wilson approved the drafting of a press release to say Nortel would be late with its financial results because of the likely need to restate them a second time. Before approving the release, however, he needed to talk with his CEO.

Dunn had not been invited to the board session. He was in Augusta, Ga., playing golf with his son David. Wilson and Cleghorn reached Dunn while he was en route to the local airport. "Can you return tonight?" Wilson said. "We need to talk." Dunn arrived that evening and stopped by Wilson's Oakville office. "We discussed whether to fire Beatty and Gollogly," Wilson said at trial. "The audit committee decided to put them on leave and (Dunn) agreed with that."

Three days later, a Saturday, Gollogly got a call at home from Nortel counsel Nick DeRoma who suggested he should get a lawyer and that Nortel would help arrange that.

When Gollogly asked why he needed a lawyer, DeRoma didn't answer. The following day, Bill

Donovan, Nortel's head of human resources, called to tell Gollogly to report to Dunn first thing Monday morning.

Everyone understood the board's distaste for having to restate again, but Gollogly felt he had done as much as he could to fix the mess created on his predecessors' watch. Indeed, his efforts to clean up Nortel's balance sheet often put him at odds with Beatty and Dunn, who had been key finance executives for years. When Dunn, without preamble, told him that he had been placed on paid leave, Gollogly couldn't help himself and said: "*I've* been suspended?" He walked out. A few minutes later it was Beatty's turn. He, too, was shocked at the turn of events.

The revelations that day that Gollogly and Beatty had been put on paid leave prompted a 19-per-cent drop in the company's share price. Two days later, shareholders launched the class-action lawsuit Nortel would later settle for $575 million in cash and $2 billion in shares.

6

A Lame-Duck CEO

Six days after Dunn put his top financial guns on leave, he gathered himself for another grilling by Wilmer Cutler's two top investigators, Wertheimer and McLucas. Dunn had told his lawyers what to expect, but they didn't quite believe him until they saw it for themselves.

"It was much more aggressive and accusatory than I had expected," Thomas Heintzman testified. "Ms. Wertheimer was civil but it was as though she had her own view of the world, which she was putting to Mr. Dunn, rather than saying 'Did this occur and did that occur?'"

Heintzman, one of McCarthy Tétrault's most senior partners, and Junior Sirivar, a litigation associate with the same firm, were the hosts of this unusual session which took place at the law firm's headquarters in the heart of Toronto's financial district. It was a Sunday, and the TD Tower was quiet. Also present in Dunn's corner were two U.S. attorneys – Larry Iason and Rich Albert – experienced in SEC proceedings.

Heintzman said Wertheimer led the questioning but that McLucas "would weigh in in sort of an aggressive tone every once in a while." The lawyer also observed that neither Wertheimer nor McLucas took notes and "I was not aware of anyone else taking notes." Heintzman meant from the Wilmer Cutler side; his colleague, Sirivar, was jotting down plenty of words.

But there was a problem, in fact, a few of them.

The first was that there had been very little time to prepare for the meeting. Although Wertheimer had emailed some material to Larry Iason several days in advance, it was blocked by Iason's spam filter and wasn't retrieved until after the meeting. Sirivar had gathered some paper files from bankers' boxes stored in Nortel's data room but wasn't sure of their relevance.

As Wertheimer began questioning Dunn, Sirivar discovered a second difficulty. Both principals spoke extremely quickly, often simultaneously. "Too many people were talking at the same time and talking quicker than I could write," Sirivar said.

The complexity of the subject matter, combined with the length of the session – some five or six hours – didn't help. "I stopped trying to even capture that because it was interfering with my ability to capture what was being said," Sirivar testified.

What was being said, though, was troubling. All day long, Wertheimer pushed documents in front of Dunn and asked him to comment or explain. She referred to their first meeting several weeks earlier when, she alleged, Dunn had acknowledged that his finance group had added reserves or provisions to turn a fourth-quarter profit into the loss that had been predicted. "No, I never said that," Dunn replied, clearly irritated. "What I said was, 'we almost made a profit and from where we came, that was pretty significant."

Wertheimer spent a lot of time on the 303, querying Dunn about why his staff maintained unnecessary reserves on Nortel's balance sheet. Wertheimer showed him emails that she said suggested finance employees were discussing the release of reserves to meet earnings targets.

Dunn questioned how any Nortel accountant would have permitted reserves to remain on the balance sheet if they weren't justified. "It makes no sense," he told Wertheimer.

The Wilmer Cutler lawyer also showed Dunn several earnings forecasts – prepared by mid-level finance manager Brian Harrison – which would occupy a prominent place in the 2012 criminal trial.

Wertheimer suggested Nortel's finance group was using these to identify potential shortfalls in earnings that would have to be made up by manipulating the balance sheet. Dunn disagreed, noting it would be inappropriate to meet targets in such a manner.

Dunn was bothered by Wertheimer's logic. Just because the first two quarters of 2003 turned out to be profitable, it didn't follow that the accounting was fraudulent. And, there was a good reason Dunn's finance team tried to forecast the movement of reserves. If Nortel did achieve quarterly profits, the company was required to pay out certain bonuses. This, in turn, meant the company had to set aside reserves to cover them. When the final results were known, Nortel would adjust the level of reserves accordingly.

The issue, as would become clear at trial, was not that Nortel's executives tracked earnings forecasts, or set aside reserves. It was whether the accounting associated with this activity was done properly. Judge Frank Marrocco ruled that it was.

"It is not contrary to the criminal law to attempt to manage the affairs of a corporation to achieve a financial target," he wrote. "The question is whether, in attempting to achieve the targeted result, those responsible for preparation of the corporation's financial results cause the financial statements to misrepresent the corporation's financial results." The accused, he added, had not done so.

§

Dunn was a lame duck CEO, indeed had been for months. The Wilmer Cutler investigation was moving relentlessly down a path he couldn't control and the directors and auditors seemed content to let the investigation play out.

This was all the more surprising given the detailed information now coming available to the Wilmer Cutler investigators. One day after Beatty and Gollogly were put on leave, Michael McMillan, Nortel's director of consolidations, sent Wilmer Cutler a detailed review of the accounting associated with Nortel's first restatement. Two weeks later Bill Kerr – who had replaced Beatty as CFO – presented the board with an analysis of the 303, showing that the vast majority of this alleged cookie jar had been properly released before yearend 2002.

The 2012 trial would establish that the $303-million pool emerged from calculations done by Sue Shaw, a relatively junior Nortel finance employee. She had been assigned the job of analyzing Nortel's $5.2-billion mountain of liabilities. Based on information from Nortel's business units, Shaw calculated that some, totalling $303 million, were no longer necessary. Shaw testified that she had based her study on estimates and extrapolations, noting that the focus on the 303 at trial far exceeded the importance it had for her at the time.

Evidence at trial showed that nearly half – $146 million – had already been released, that is, removed from the balance sheet before Sept. 30, 2002. Another $76 million would be removed in the fourth quarter of 2002. Marrocco concluded the remainder of the $303 million had either been dealt with appropriately, or the items had been described so vaguely, they couldn't be identified.

In the days following Kerr's presentation, however, Wilmer Cutler's investigators unearthed emails that purported to show Nortel's top executives had been manipulating earnings. The Crown, which had access to the Wilmer Cutler file, would later introduce several dozen suggestive emails. But when Nortel witnesses were asked to explain, it was clear the words had been misinterpreted.

For instance, Crown attorney Robert Hubbard produced an email written by Beatty, who noted late in 2003 that it was "amnesty time" and that "from now on people will be fired for not following proper accounting practices." The inference is that Nortel staff prior to that point had not been fired for practising bad accounting. But during the trial, McMillan testified that what Beatty meant was that employees should be forthcoming about "the backdrop to the various entries" and not worry about being fired for bringing forward potentially bad news, such as mistaken assumptions underlying earlier estimates.

Hubbard also introduced a Jan. 11, 2003 email composed by Linda Mezon – then Nortel's assistant corporate controller. In it, Mezon told a colleague that Beatty was "most concerned" about the excess and obsolete accounting. "Can we look at this next week," Mezon wrote, "and then I can get Helen (Verity, Nortel's director of consolidations) to move provisions around as needed. Apparently this is straight from FAD (Frank Dunn)."

At first blush, Mezon appears to have been suggesting that Verity was free to shift accounting entries according to Dunn's wishes. However, Mezon explained that since the entry in question involved the sale of a Nortel business unit, she was concerned that the related accounting be done in the correct categories – under continuing or discontinued operations, for instance.

"We had to make sure it was in the right segment," she testified.

In his opening statement at the criminal trial, Hubbard alleged that Nortel's U.S. controller, Karen Sledge, had advised Beatty and Gollogly that results for the third quarter of 2003 were 'polluted,' meaning they had been influenced by the release of liabilities that lacked a proper trigger. Sledge denied this assertion, as did her Nortel colleagues Peter Dans and McMillan. The Crown appears to have misinterpreted the implementation of a system designed to separate liabilities without proper paperwork (which were coded) from the rest of Nortel's reserves. Nortel did this in order to prevent improper reserves from influencing the third quarter. Sledge had been making the point that until staff removed the coded liabilities, the results would be 'polluted.' Gollogly and Sledge had been trying to get the numbers right.

§

At 8:30 on the morning of April 27, 2004, Nortel's directors gathered in the company's second-floor boardroom in Brampton for what would prove another lengthy board meeting. Though the venue was just down the hall from Dunn's office, none dropped by. Five hours later, one finally did. Bob Brown, the chief executive of CAE Inc., one of Canada's most celebrated aerospace firms, emerged to tell Dunn, "It's not going well in there, Frank, but whatever happens, keep your chin up."

Late in the afternoon, a delegation of three marched from the boardroom to Dunn's office – Wilson, Cleghorn and Bob Ingram, a pharmaceutical firm executive. The conversation was brief. When he learned he was being fired for cause, along with Beatty and Gollogly, Dunn was momentarily stunned. What cause?

They gave him three.

The first, according to Wilson, related to "tone at the top" – Dunn had set a poor example for his finance group.

Cleghorn added that Nortel's first restatement was now in the process of being redone and that Dunn, as CEO, had accountability for that. Dunn replied, angrily, that he had voluntarily stepped away from that analysis because of his previous job as chief financial officer and that it was, in fact, Cleghorn who had had responsibility for overseeing the initial restatement. The audit committee chairman said nothing.

The third cause? Dunn demanded. Sarbanes-Oxley, Wilson said. When Dunn offered that he had done good work for the company over many years, Wilson nodded in agreement. Wilson would later say Dunn helped restore the company to profitability, but in Dunn's office that day, when he started to say more, Ingram interrupted him and pulled him away. The meeting was over.

Dunn wouldn't have believed it then, but worse was to come.

7

Texas Says 'No'

The days immediately following his firing were a thick haze for Dunn. It wasn't just the shock of losing his job, it was what this entailed. As CEO of a $10-billion-a-year global corporation, he had been on the road four days out of five, touring Nortel facilities from China to Texas, visiting key customers and checking out competitors at telecommunications trade shows. It was a gruelling lifestyle, albeit one with ample compensations – a million-dollar annual salary and bonus, a corporate jet at his disposal, and the prestige that came with running what was still one of the country's most valuable corporations.

Overnight, all this disappeared. Equally torturous was having to watch his successor, Bill Owens, make a show of cleaning up Nortel. Owens appointed a chief ethics officer and demanded that the firm's executives return the multimillion-dollar bonuses they had earned on Dunn's watch. When some resisted, Owens threatened to make life difficult for them. Owens also told the director of investigations at the SEC that Nortel would spend whatever was required to correct its accounting misdeeds.

Dunn spent the first part of May with Junior Sirivar, the McCarthy Tétrault lawyer who had accompanied him to his second interview with Wertheimer.

Dunn had been taking copious notes of his meetings with Wertheimer, Wilson and others. He and Sirivar compiled a detailed timeline. Part of it was to prepare for all the litigation coming Dunn's way. But for Dunn, there was a more personal purpose as well. He was trying to figure out just what had happened. For the next nine years, he transferred the energy he had devoted to running Nortel to investigating the circumstances that had led to his firing. It was a quest that led him to consume most of the four million documents that would ultimately be disclosed to his lawyers.

§

The legal forces arrayed against Dunn were many. A federal grand jury in Texas had issued a subpoena for documents from Nortel shortly after he was fired. In August 2004, the RCMP announced they had begun a formal investigation of Nortel's accounting. The impetus was powerful – Nortel had sacked its top financial executives for cause. Although the company wasn't specific, the RCMP believed it was safe in assuming serious transgressions had taken place. The U.S. Securities and Exchange Commission and the Ontario Securities Commission – the agencies responsible for regulating the stock exchanges – had begun a probe of Nortel's accounting after the firm put Beatty and Gollogly on leave.

Nortel co-operated fully. Under the command of Owens, the company forwarded the conclusions of the Wilmer Cutler investigation and related documents. The Wilmer Cutler-inspired tale of how the fired executives manipulated Nortel's balance sheet to create desired earnings thus became the starting point for the criminal and civil proceedings. It would take a crush of countervailing evidence at the 2012 trial before the real story would take hold.

There had been warning signs the case was weak. For one thing, the allegations of wrongdoing were surprisingly imprecise, starting with the civil fraud charges levelled against Dunn, Beatty, Gollogly and other members of Nortel's finance team. The SEC and OSC told Dunn's lawyers that questions about what, exactly, constituted an illegal accounting entry were matters to be decided at trial. Dunn submitted dozens of documents in the SEC proceeding showing how the allegedly problematic accounting had been scrutinized thoroughly by Nortel's external auditors, Deloitte. Included were Deloitte's presentations to Nortel's audit committee.

Even so, three of the eight Nortel managers targeted by the SEC were quick to settle, rather than face years of expensive litigation. Craig Johnson, James Kinney and Ken Taylor – the vice-presidents respectively of Nortel's wireline, wireless and enterprise units – paid six-figure fines and moved on with their lives. However, MaryAnne Pahapill, Nortel's controller, and Douglas Hamilton, the vice-president of finance for Nortel's optical products group, declined to settle. Both challenged the SEC to give reasons why the fraud charges shouldn't be dismissed, as did Dunn and Beatty. (Gollogly's strategy, dictated by a lack of money, was simply to ignore the SEC proceedings.)

Only the three most senior executives faced the more worrisome prospect of criminal charges. Assistant U.S. Attorney for the Northern District of Texas Jeff Ansley claimed jurisdiction south of the border because one of Nortel's largest foreign offices was in Richardson, Texas, a global hub for wireless technologies.

Tellingly, Ansley gave it a pass. The lead prosecutor for the Northern District's Securities Fraud Task Force had worked major fraud cases in the U.S. Attorney's Office since 2002 and knew his way around corporate accounts. There was something he didn't like about the Nortel dossier. It wasn't just the fact that Deloitte had signed off on every significant accounting item – he knew of cases in which auditors were complicit in wrongdoing. Nor was it the complexity of the case. Ansley was also familiar with the contortions of contract accounting in major public corporations.

The difficulty lay with the potential witnesses. Nearly all the Nortel finance employees believed they had done nothing wrong.

A possible exception was Sledge, Nortel's top controller in the U.S. But even her testimony from a prosecutor's point of view was worrisome. Wertheimer had asked Sledge in February 2004 if she had participated in any accounting transactions that made her uncomfortable. Sledge allowed that one had indeed troubled her. But when examined more closely, the item in question was a quagmire that signified little – like many other accounting transactions in this case would prove to be.

Sledge said she had calculated in January 2003 that the reserve account she had created to cover fringe benefit costs for Nortel's laid-off employees in the U.S. was $37 million more than originally believed necessary. Gollogly had been furious when he learned about it. Just four months earlier Sledge had told him she expected there would be a $16-million shortfall in the fringe benefit reserve. If Sledge's revised estimate was correct, it would improve fourth-quarter earnings by $53 million, a significant amount.

Gollogly didn't like being blindsided like this and asked Sledge to double-check. In fact, he was so angry at her surprise revision, he swore at her over the phone. Soon after, he called to apologize but reminded her to check her math.

Sledge told Wertheimer that she had complied with what she considered to be Gollogly's directive. After consulting her staff, Sledge told Gollogly she would release $26 million, not $37 million. The impact would be to decrease fourth-quarter earnings by $11 million compared to her first revision.

Wertheimer – and, much later, Crown attorney Hubbard – came to see this as part of a longstanding pattern of earnings manipulation at Nortel. Gollogly's second call would be taken as evidence of inappropriate pressure from head office. Hubbard alleged that the accounting change involving fringe benefits was one of many entries that Nortel made at the last minute to prevent an unexpected fourth-quarter profit. Dunn had earlier predicted a loss, the Crown attorney noted, so a loss there would be.

However, the fringe benefit transaction had a much different look when subjected to scrutiny at the trial. Sledge, who once dated Gollogly, declined to say under cross-examination just what it was about Gollogly's request and the resulting change in accounting that had made her uncomfortable. Also, Gollogly's defence counsel introduced evidence to explain why he had queried Sledge's original entry.

In September 2002, when Sledge told Gollogly to expect a $16-million shortfall in the fringe benefit reserve, she explained that employees on layoff notice were using more medical benefits than expected. However, evidence at trial showed that two of Sledge's employees – both new to the fringe benefit account – had missed some four months' worth of data related to severance projections. This provided part of the explanation for why the reserve several months later seemed too high. Then, Deloitte discovered that the cost of some of the fringe benefits had been double counted as a restructuring expense. This mistake was fixed through a series of quarterly adjustments in 2003.

It's not known if Ansley had this kind of detail at his fingertips early in 2008. A source familiar with the Texas investigation said Ansley's office interviewed a former colleague of Sledge, in part to determine whether Gollogly applied inappropriate pressure to change the level of fringe reserves. Shortly after the interview, Ansley decided not to pursue a criminal case against Nortel or its top executives. If there was to be a criminal prosecution of Nortel's executives, the RCMP would have to take it on.

§

In the spring of 2008, four full years into its investigation, the RCMP hadn't gotten very far. Indeed, their lack of progress in analyzing the evidence was shocking. Nortel had turned over several million documents but just 200,000 had been imported into Supertext, the RCMP's document management system. And many of these items, if not most, had been selected by Wilmer Cutler. It was still very much the Washington lawyers' story.

RCMP Sgt. Rafael Alvarado had attempted to import everything into a single, searchable database with the help of Concordance software, but he was unable to do it in a manner that properly linked associated documents.

To rectify this massive deficiency, the RCMP asked Nortel to redisclose what it termed the core documents.

The request went out on May 6, just six weeks before the RCMP would lay charges against Dunn, Beatty and Gollogly. One of Nortel's U.S. law firms, Shearman & Stirling LLP, had collected and scanned the mountain of paper and electronic documents. What was being proposed by the RCMP was to tweak the original data so that families of documents would remain attached to each other.

But a dispute arose between the RCMP and Nortel over who should pay for the re-disclosure and the two sides dropped the matter. In any case, such a move would benefit mainly the defence, as became clear on June 11. On that day, just eight days before Dunn, Beatty and Gollogly were charged, the police and Crown met and determined "not to give the defence a better system than we had."

Even if Nortel had complied with the RCMP's request to re-disclose, it would have involved only one-third of the four million documents. The RCMP was interested mainly in documents created between March 31, 2002 and July 31, 2004, the period in which the crimes allegedly took place. This omitted emails and other presentations that would have shed light on the reasons why many of the problematic accounting entries were set up, and on Nortel's subsequent analysis of the various restatements.

Defence lawyers for Dunn, Beatty and Gollogly wanted to search the documents in their own way, and not be forced to rely on a portion of evidence selected mainly by Wilmer Cutler. They sought a ruling in late December 2009 from Ontario Superior Court Justice Cary Boswell, who had sympathy for their position.

"The status quo is such that, should it continue until trial," Boswell wrote, "the Crown would have all of the documents it says are relevant to its case sorted, organized and quickly and fully searchable in Supertext." In sharp contrast, he noted, the defence would be "buried in millions of images that no one has ever assessed as to relevance."

Accordingly, Boswell ordered the Crown and Nortel to deliver a full Concordance database searchable by key fields including date, author, recipient, subject matter and source. This ruling came a full 18 months *after* the RCMP had laid charges. But more astonishingly, this legal sideshow revealed the RCMP had arrested Dunn, Beatty and Gollogly in 2008 after reviewing only a sliver of the potential evidence. The trial would show the Crown misinterpreted many of the documents it did examine.

8

The Fall of a Telecom Titan

Any solace the former Nortel executives took from Boswell's 2009 ruling was fleeting. At this stage in the proceedings they had been branded as fraud artists by the RCMP, abandoned by friends, and forbidden by the terms of their bail from talking with former colleagues. Dozens of people were on the list of prohibited contacts.

But perhaps most difficult of all, the accused had to watch from a distance as the company they helped build – and believed they had been on the verge of saving – descended into bankruptcy.

The first clue Nortel was in peril came Sept. 17, 2008, three months after Dunn, Beatty and Gollogly were released on bail. Company CEO Mike Zafirovski – the former Motorola executive hired in 2005 to lead a 'historic' turnaround – announced that Nortel's revenues were sliding in response to the global credit crisis. He predicted the company's sales of telecommunications gear and services would barely top $10 billion in 2008, about $1 billion less than expected. Zafirovski froze salaries and reduced the firm's use of contract workers and professional services. In November he trimmed the firm's workforce by another 1,300 – the fourth big layoff since 2006.

Although Nortel had more than $2 billion in cash, it was dispersed widely through its many entities. The company was also carrying more than $4 billion in long-term debt. Zafirovski had to start thinking about emergency sources of capital. He met with key officials from the federal departments of Industry and Finance. After the Conservative government was re-elected Oct. 14, he lobbied Industry Minister Tony Clement and Transport Minister John Baird.

The sessions did not go well and at least some of the blame lay with Zafirovski. Nortel never produced a compelling rationale for its claim on taxpayers' money. Zafirovski floated half-a-dozen scenarios, each supported by different assumptions about which Nortel division would be divested, and how fast the economy would recover. Government officials were confused about the firm's strategy. Desperate for some cash, any cash, Nortel whittled its original request for $1 billion down to $500 million. The Conservatives weren't in a mood to be generous.

Working against Zafirovski was the feeling among key members of cabinet that Nortel had only itself to blame for its predicament. Not only had the firm sacked three executives for not playing by the rules, it had made a mess of its chances to redeem itself. After the firm fired Dunn, it installed two CEOs in succession – Owens and Zafirovski – unfamiliar with the telecommunications industry. Owens concentrated on ethics and Zafirovski told every customer of his plans to transform Nortel into the most efficient maker of telecom gear.

Customers didn't especially care about either priority. They wanted to know what Nortel could do to improve their telecommunications networks. And, while the company was still very good in certain aspects of the industry – Internet voice technology, voice and data networks for corporations, fibre-optic gear and CDMA (code division multiple access) wireless networks – it was an also-ran in too many other parts of its business.

Sweden's Ericsson dominated wireless technologies while Cisco and Juniper Networks were the class of the field in building Internet routers. Nortel was also being squeezed at the low-cost end of the spectrum by a pair of new rivals from China – Huawei Technologies and ZTE. This became apparent as early as 2005, when Huawei edged out Nortel in a multibillion-dollar procurement sponsored by Britain's global carrier, BT PLC.

It's no accident that Nortel lost a lot of ground to rivals from 2004 through 2007 when it was so distracted by seemingly endless accounting issues. The firm coped with constant requests from securities regulators, RCMP inspectors and forensic accountants. During the peak of the accounting examination, several hundred outside professionals were combing through the company's books – as well as consuming Nortel's dwindling cash reserves. One company director present during most of the two plus years Wilmer Cutler did its probe notes that the drawn out presentations from the investigators and auditors at board meetings was a tremendous distraction, "giving us relatively little time to address the fundamental issues facing the corporation."

On Jan. 9, 2009, 11 Nortel directors gathered near Toronto Pearson International Airport to consider whether to file for bankruptcy protection. The company still had $2.4 billion cash on hand, but little more than one-third of it was held in North America and only $176 million in Canada. Set against this was a $107-million debt interest payment due in six days.

Zafirovski told the directors that more cash was on the way, either through a federal government bailout or the sale of one of Nortel's business units. But the CEO's credibility was waning.

More importantly, the financial world seemed to be descending into a black pit of despair. Stock markets in North America had lost more than 40 per cent of their value and it was not clear whether the bottom had been reached. Even if Zafirovski could find a buyer for one of Nortel's business units, it was doubtful he'd receive much money for it. Nortel's suppliers, worried about whether the company would pay them for goods and services already delivered, were demanding cash up front. On Jan. 13, Nortel's directors voted to hold the firm's creditors at bay. They filed for bankruptcy the following day.

The idea was to use the protection of the courts to reorganize the firm. Nortel could lay off employees without having to pay millions in severance. It could take more time to sort out what divisions to sell and to whom – and what parts of the business to keep. Nortel would re-emerge later in the year a leaner, more competitive firm.

But to succeed such a strategy required a leader with energy, someone who, through sheer force of will, could hold the core pieces of the organization together. The rebuilding effort demanded a CEO familiar with the traits that had once made Nortel great, in particular its willingness to place huge bets on developing the right technologies at the right time. Nortel had done so in the late 1970s by being the first company to develop a complete family of digital telecommunications gear; this was the basis of its transformation into a global corporation. In the 1990s, Nortel was the first to build 40 gigabits-per-second optical transmission gear, which became the standard for carrying Internet traffic during the tech boom and lit a fuse under the corporation's share price until late in 2000.

The trick for corporations that achieve miracles like this is to reinvest profits in new inventions or businesses that also make money one day.

Many employ dozens of specialists to work on blue sky projects in the hope of producing one or two giant hits. Nortel had a special knack for pushing the boundaries of physics in its labs. The tragedy lay in its inability to commercialize more of it. It's impossible to know whether Nortel, absent the accounting problems, would have succeeded. But certainly the firm would have been in much stronger financial position to withstand the shock of recession in 2008 and 2009, regardless of who was running it.

On June 22, 2009, Nortel announced it would begin the process of selling off its businesses, starting with its wireless technologies. By July 1, 2010, the company had unloaded all of them for $3 billion – and sold its patents for $4.5 billion. Little more than a year earlier, Zafirovski had estimated the patents might fetch several hundred million dollars. The buyers of the patents, which included Apple Inc. and Research in Motion Ltd., understood more clearly the value of what had been created in Nortel's labs.

§

Dunn too knew what had been lost. He had joined Nortel in 1976, just a few months after the company unveiled Digital World, its high-risk effort to produce a complete family of digital switches, the computers of the telecommunications world. In advertising for engineering talent, Nortel – then known as Northern

Telecom – wanted potential employees to understand what was at stake. "Northern is in the midst of the most ambitious digital switching program ever undertaken," the ad proclaimed. "We want you to be part of it."

That was vintage Nortel. Early in 2004, before he met Laura Wertheimer and the rest of her colleagues from Wilmer Cutler, Dunn had entertained hope he could recoup some of the firm's lost glory.

With recovery would come a steady stream of profits to strengthen Nortel's balance sheet and secure its research budget. This part was no pipe dream – the company recorded profits of nearly half a billion dollars during the fourth quarter of 2003.

It was why Dunn found it quite easy to justify rich bonuses to his executive team and ordinary employees. It was also why he was so distressed at the position he found himself in the day he lost his job.

9

A Deposed Prince Loses His Palace

Anyone who knew Dunn then would have been surprised to discover how thin his financial cushion really was. He was building a monster dream home in Oakville's wealthiest enclave. The two-storey stone mansion – all 10,800 square feet of it – was set on a 1.7-acre lakefront property with a boathouse, boat slip and swimming pool. The day he was fired, the house was still at the drywall stage and the grounds had not been landscaped. Dunn's plans, though, were grandiose and included a home theatre, exercise room, sauna, billiards room, communications centre and a virtual golf room that would allow Frank and his friends to play any one of 50 computer-simulated golf courses.

Dunn had acquired the property for $4.3 million Cdn in August 2002 and shared details of the construction with colleagues. At the time, he and his wife, Nancy, lived nearby in a home at 91 Bel Air Dr., which was valued at about $3 million Cdn. The idea had been to sell the Bel Air property when the palace at 2100 Lakeshore Rd. E. was finished.

As ex-CEO, Dunn knew almost instantly his dream home wasn't going to happen. His $825,000 annual salary was gone. And, unbeknownst to all but a few colleagues and Nortel's directors, he had declined nearly $8 million worth of bonuses earned in 2003. This wasn't entirely for selfless reasons; Wilmer Cutler investigators had recommended withholding bonuses from all Nortel executives until the investigation of Nortel's accounting was complete – a suggestion that didn't sit well with Dunn.

He engaged in a long, sometimes bitter debate with Nortel's directors over the pros and cons of waiting for Wilmer Cutler's conclusions. Nortel's board of directors at the time had approved several bonus programs – some were short-term in nature while others attempted to reinforce longer-term corporate goals such as achieving a certain level of profit compared to revenue over various periods.

At Dunn's urging, the board late in 2002 launched a bonus plan that would reward nearly all Nortel employees after the company recorded a single quarter of profit. However, the 40-plus top managers would receive their bonuses only in stages, provided Nortel continued recording profits over a full year.

The company's top 18 executives were also eligible to receive units of stock under a multi-year program that began in 2001 and was renewed in 2003. It was this bonus plan that triggered the fiercest battle between Dunn and the board. To end the impasse, Dunn and Beatty volunteered to forgo their bonuses provided the other executives got theirs. The board approved a $27.3-million payout for 16 executives, excluding Dunn and

Beatty. The previous year, all 18 executives earned nearly $14 million under the first phase of the stock unit program. Dunn received $2.2 million, Beatty earned $831,000 and Gollogly was awarded $432,000. Gollogly also received $620,000 under the second phase of the plan.

The 2004 payout proved a fleeting victory for the 16 executives. After Dunn, Beatty and Gollogly were fired new CEO Owens persuaded the rest of his management team to return their bonuses, then sued the three sacked executives to try to reclaim their awards.

Although Dunn declined the second stock unit payment, he should still have had sizeable resources. In 2000, at the height of the telecom boom, he exercised his right to acquire Nortel shares for gross proceeds of $14.8 million Cdn. But he kept most of the shares rather than sell them and trigger taxes owing. And, thanks in part to the events with which he had been associated, the value of those shares plummeted.

Then there was the looming legal fight. The instant Nortel fired him, the company terminated payment of his legal fees. Dunn learned that Chubb Insurance Co. of Canada – Nortel's carrier – was covering barely half his legal bills.

The value of his real estate assets had also been compromised. Dunn had taken a line of credit against the Bel Air property to finance the construction of his dream home. When he put the unfinished property up for sale – the initial asking price was nearly $11 million Cdn – he discovered that potential buyers knew very well who owned it, and what his circumstances were. Dunn settled for a price of $9 million Cdn, allowing him to pay off his line of credit and leaving him with several million dollars.

His net proceeds shrank quickly. In 2007, he and his colleagues were charged with accounting fraud by the

U.S. Securities and Exchange Commission and the Ontario Securities Commission. The RCMP followed up with criminal charges a year later. A year after that, Dunn filed a motion to stay the SEC proceeding, citing poverty.

In it, Dunn noted that the SEC case would cost him anywhere from $3 million to $5 million, depending on the length of the civil trial.

The motion also claimed that defending against criminal charges in Canada would cost between $2.8 million Cdn and $3.9 million Cdn, and that he'd already advanced about $2.1 million Cdn. This included some $700,000 Cdn lent to him by former Nortel colleagues, including former CEO John Roth and former chief marketing officer Ian Craig. Against these future legal bills, Dunn had roughly $500,000 Cdn in cash and securities, and a $1.5-million Cdn credit line secured against his half of the Bel Air home. Dunn said he had already drawn $786,000 Cdn against that line of credit.

Within months that home, too, was gone. He and Nancy sold it in December 2009 for $2.75 million Cdn – again, less than expected. Dunn was now betting everything on an ongoing lawsuit against Chubb to try to force the insurance firm to pay at least 90 per cent of the legal bills for him and Beatty. (Gollogly later became a beneficiary of this fight.)

Dunn lost the first phase of the war early in 2009 when Ontario Superior Court Justice Colin Campbell ruled that Chubb was within its rights to deny Dunn and Beatty coverage for certain legal expenses. The former Nortel executives won their appeal of that ruling, after arguing that language in the agreements meant Chubb's coverage applied more broadly. The Ontario Court of Appeal kicked the case back to Campbell to consider the relevant section in Chubb's policy more carefully. Campbell recused himself in favour of Judge Donald

Cameron, who ruled on April 23, 2010, that Chubb should bear 90 per cent of the legal costs incurred by the Nortel executives.

Dunn and Beatty couldn't celebrate just yet, however, because Chubb challenged the decision. Finally, on Jan. 18, 2011, the Ontario Court of Appeal upheld Cameron's ruling. Chubb would have to pay 90 per cent. But even here there was a catch. The decision applied retroactively only to the date of Cameron's 2010 ruling.

Dunn was out of pocket for the legal costs associated with his criminal defence in 2008 and 2009 – in excess of $1.5 million. But now he, Beatty and Gollogly could challenge the most serious of the charges – that they had orchestrated a clever conspiracy to cook the books under the noses of hundreds of onsite auditors from Deloitte.

10

Groundhog Day in Toronto

The proceedings in courtroom 4-10 felt at times like a screening of the movie Groundhog Day, in which the character played by Bill Murray discovers that each new day is Feb. 2 all over again. From Jan. 16 to June 26, 2012, the Crown led 17 witnesses over carefully prepared ground. Against the backdrop of sirens emanating constantly from Toronto's University Avenue, each offered a slightly different perspective on an accounting transaction, email or meeting that took place in 2002 or 2003.

With each new witness, Crown attorney Robert Hubbard returned to the same entries, again and again. So often did he refer to certain parts of Nortel's balance sheet that he resorted to shorthand – the 303 and the 189, in reference to alleged 'cookie jars,' and the fourth-quarter 'callout,' which described alleged efforts by Nortel finance employees to improperly solicit last-minute liabilities in 2002.

"That Nortel's books, records and financial statements were false is beyond question," Hubbard declared during his final arguments. "The accused knew Nortel's financial 'reality' but they lied about it."

The accused had near-complete confidence the charges of fraud would be seen as the product of a witch hunt. Not surprisingly, they hated every minute of the Crown's show.

The former executives watched, silent, from the left side of the courtroom, arranged in the hierarchy of the jobs they used to fill. Dunn and his lawyers from McCarthy Tétrault occupied the front two benches. Beatty, the former CFO, sat further back, accompanied by Gregory Lafontaine, an experienced criminal lawyer with his own practice and something of a street fighter.

Michael Gollogly, the former controller, observed proceedings from the back, just in front of the benches reserved for the public. His lawyers, Sharon Lavine and Robin McKechney, were partners with Greenspan Humphrey Lavine, a boutique law firm well known in the Toronto area thanks to the high profile of Brian Greenspan, one of its founding partners.

The public benches, which seat about 50, were usually occupied only by a few. The material was too dense, the subject matter too dry. Most days there were two or three journalists, friends and family of the accused – though when a Deloitte partner testified, a phalanx of lawyers presented itself. More surprisingly, when Hubbard finished examining a witness nearly all the journalists left. The detailed cross-examinations that so quickly undermined the Crown's case went largely unreported by the country's biggest-circulation newspapers.

When the court recessed, the accused and lawyers left through the north door. During the early weeks of the trial, opposing counsel bantered easily. Toward the end, conversations were more strained. It wasn't just the stress of such a long, complicated proceeding. Defence lawyers were increasingly annoyed by the Crown's tendency to continue arguing points that had been thoroughly discredited by hard evidence.

"The Crown in large measure has not even attempted to address a very substantial body of evidence of innocence, choosing to proceed as though it simply does not exist," Lafontaine said during his final argument.

"It's been a case where the Crown has called witnesses liars and perjurers when their evidence does not fit within or fall into line with the Crown's theory of guilty."

Indeed, the profound weakness of Hubbard's case was evident the moment the defence began cross-examining his witnesses.

§

David Porter is a serious and careful litigator, as befits a senior partner at McCarthy Tétrault – one of Toronto's most established law firms. Yet not even his quiet monotone could disguise the importance of the document he held in his hand on Feb. 2, 2012. It was the ninth day of the trial and Porter had been cross-examining Brian Harrison, the Crown's first witness and a former member of Nortel's finance team.

Porter was showing Harrison part of an 18-page PDF, dated July 15, 2003. It had been prepared by three senior members of Deloitte's Complex Accounting and Transaction Expertise Group – Diana De Acetis, Peter Chant and Chris Allen. In it, the auditors considered in some detail the six accounting transactions that together had improved Nortel's earnings by $80 million during the first quarter of 2003.

The entries, and what they represented, were absolutely vital to the Crown's case. Hubbard alleged the six items had been taken from a $189-million 'cookie jar' of liabilities that had been kept on the company's balance sheet as a tool for managing earnings.

Hubbard asserted the accused had improperly removed the $80 million to transform a first-quarter loss into a pro forma profit of $40 million. This result, in turn, triggered $73 million worth of 'return to profitability' bonuses for staff and $46 million worth of 'success' bonuses for the wider executive group.

But as Porter read portions of the Deloitte memo aloud, it was apparent to nearly everyone in the courtroom that Nortel's auditors had concluded the bonuses were legitimate. According to the auditors' calculations, the bonuses would have been payable whether or not the $80 million was factored in – in which case, what was the motive for the alleged fraud?

A few days earlier, under examination by the Crown, Harrison had testified that had Nortel not released the $80 million in liabilities, there would have been no profit. But Porter, reading from the Deloitte document, pointed out the formula for calculating bonuses wasn't as simple as it appeared. It was based, he said, on pro forma earnings, which excluded items such as stock-based compensation expenses, special charges and gains on the buyback of bonds. As Porter went through the memo's explanation of the bonus calculation, Harrison responded "that's correct" 12 times in just a few minutes.

Porter then reached the key point. Nortel's board of directors had decided in April 2003 that the bonus calculation was to be based on Nortel's more generous 2002 definition of pro forma earnings "for greater certainty." Had the $80 million never been removed, there would still have been a significant pro forma profit, Deloitte concluded. Harrison agreed he had failed to appreciate the full complexity of the pro forma profit calculation during his testimony before the Crown. "I wasn't taking into account these earlier adjustments," Harrison said.

The Crown and its forensic accountants had ignored this vital point – a surprising omission given that they had copies of the document in their files. Perhaps Hubbard had been hoping the defence wouldn't discover the De Acetis memo, which originated from Deloitte's desk files but was not produced to the Crown until Dec. 23, 2011, and somewhat later to the defence. Or maybe Hubbard had not expected Marrocco to give it quite so much weight.

Nor was that the only damage done to the Crown's case by the De Acetis memo. Later in the trial, defence attorney Harry Underwood introduced details from the first part of the document. These showed that the Deloitte auditors had considered each of the six items that comprised the $80 million and concluded the accounting had been done according to generally accepted accounting principles.

Taken in its entirety, the De Acetis document captured Deloitte's view that the accounting had been correct, the bonuses appropriate.

That was far from the end of the bad news for the Crown. Just two weeks after introducing the Deloitte analysis, Porter blew apart another piece of Hubbard's case. He entered a memo written by Deloitte partner Karen Keilty dated March 15, 2004 – the same day Nortel placed Beatty and Gollogly on leave. The document contained a list of more than $400 million worth of liabilities that lacked paperwork and had been examined by Deloitte the previous year in connection with its audit of Nortel's 2002 numbers. Keilty was responding to a request for the list from John Cawthorne, Deloitte's top auditor on the Nortel file.

On the list were transactions that formed part of the 303, the 189 and the Wilmer Cutler 14 – the starting points for allegations that Nortel's accounting had been dirty. It undermined the entire notion that Nortel's executives had improperly maintained cookie jars: Deloitte and Nortel had been dealing with the problematic accounting entries long before Wilmer Cutler and the other independent investigators arrived on the scene. They had been trying to get the numbers right.

11

The Conspiracy That Made
No Sense

Hubbard was a relative latecomer to the Nortel litigation. In the summer of 2009 – his 32nd year as a prosecutor – he was riding high after securing a victory in the high-profile case involving the proprietors of Livent Inc., a Toronto theatre production company. Livent founders Garth Drabinsky and Marvin Gottlieb were sentenced in August to seven years and six years, respectively, for accounting fraud, though the terms were reduced on appeal by two years each.

Hubbard's fellow Crown attorney Sandy Tse had been managing the Nortel file to that point. But Hubbard, with more experience quarterbacking complex fraud trials, was the more logical one to take on the fight. The University of Toronto law school grad inserted himself into the picture just as some defence counsel were entertaining hope the charges against their clients might actually be dropped. The evidence had always seemed thin and the RCMP seemed to be having great difficulty managing the extremely voluminous file.

In 2009 and again in 2011 Dunn's lawyer, Porter, forwarded to the Crown hundreds more documents – most to do with Deloitte's extensive knowledge of the allegedly troublesome accounting issues.

The Crown, in turn, sent the documents to its accounting expert, John Douglas. The hope was that once the Crown saw the truth behind the numbers, it would finally understand there had been no crime.

At first, Hubbard's influence was behind the scenes. Tse's name was attached to Judge Cary Boswell's ruling on Dec. 21, 2009, when the Crown lost its bid to prevent proper disclosure of all four million documents to the defence. Tse also signed the revision of charges on Jan. 28, 2010, when the Crown extended the time frame for some of the seven charges from Jan. 1, 2002 back to Jan. 1, 2000.

It soon became apparent Hubbard was running the show – defence lawyers noticed a sudden hardening of resolve. In February 2010 Hubbard brought a motion to dismiss Dunn's counsel – McCarthy Tétrault – on an alleged conflict of interest. The firm had been representing Deloitte outside Canada on an unrelated matter. Hubbard also sought to enter into evidence the summaries written by Wilmer Cutler following its interviews of Beatty, Gollogly and Dunn in 2004.

The Crown lost both motions. On the first matter, Boswell ruled there was no qualifying conflict of interest. In a second pre-trial ruling, Justice Ian Nordheimer declared the Wilmer Cutler memos inadmissible because they failed the requirement for reliability. Wertheimer and her colleagues had not taped the proceedings, and the summaries contained impressions and thoughts more closely associated with client-solicitor privilege.

After Nordheimer's ruling, Hubbard warned defence counsel he would call as witnesses the lawyers who had accompanied Dunn and Beatty in the Wilmer Cutler interviews. (Gollogly took all three of his grillings without the help of counsel.) One way or another, Hubbard wanted the court to hear the investigators' allegations. He had no patience for the view that perhaps Wilmer Cutler's opinions of Nortel's accounting were debatable or wrong.

In June 2010, Douglas, the Crown's forensic accountant, produced his analysis of Nortel's 2003 accounting: while he questioned some of Deloitte's judgment, the report confirmed the auditor's extensive involvement in Nortel's decision-making.

Dunn's lawyers forwarded a copy of the report to Nordheimer, prompting the judge to ask Hubbard how he intended to make his case. The Crown attorney said he would argue some of Deloitte's auditors should not have signed off on certain items – whether through incompetence or in the role of co-conspirator was immaterial to him.

"Even if Deloitte or others knew about or acquiesced to the accuseds' false filings," Hubbard said in his closing statement, "this could not exculpate (exonerate) the accused. The accused had direct responsibility for the filings of the false financial statements and attendant documents."

How did he know they were false? Wilmer Cutler had said they were.

§

Hubbard's strategy – which was to infer fraud from the fact of a restatement – was a first. Never before had a criminal court in Canada considered this notion. It's easy to see why not. For starters the accounting profession makes allowance for restatements on the understanding that it's impossible to get the numbers perfect in large corporations. Auditors rely on a concept called materiality. Each quarter, based on the company's projected earnings and revenues, auditors determine a materiality threshold below which errors are considered too small to worry about. But if errors become large, as they did at Nortel, they must either be explained in a footnote to the earnings statements (as they were in the first quarter of 2003) or be restated. The year Nortel restated its numbers, hundreds of other public corporations did the same thing.

A restatement on its own is not evidence of fraud. However, Nortel's second restatement – the one announced on Jan. 10, 2005 – had been influenced heavily by Wilmer Cutler. Accordingly, Hubbard reasoned, these numbers had a special character. They represented Wilmer Cutler's efforts to make right the first restatement, which the outside investigators alleged had been fraudulent.

It was an ambitious theory but it failed the test of inspection. Marrocco ruled that the differences between the two restatements could be attributed to the fact auditors were measuring different things according to different thresholds. Not only that, but the accounting reflected differing interpretations by Deloitte.

"The restatement of individual accrued liability balances occurred for a variety of reasons," Marrocco ruled. "It is not safe to generalize. The specifics of each restated balance have to be looked at in order to see what inferences they support. The first restatement was validated."

Indeed, the Crown was very much aware of the difficulty of establishing fraud item by item. The facts just weren't there.

By 2011, the Crown and the RCMP had had seven years in which to try to prove the allegations made by Wilmer Cutler – namely, that the company's top executives had improperly engineered earnings to gain access to their bonuses. Investigators had interviewed dozens of Nortel employees and several from Deloitte. They had employed forensic accountants and studied hundreds of thousands of documents and emails. Yet, despite threatening several potential witnesses with criminal charges if they did not co-operate, the Crown and the RCMP still had no case.

The police agency's heavy reliance on Wilmer Cutler's documentation seemed clear late in 2005 when Gollogly took the unusual step of volunteering to be interviewed by RCMP Const. Debbie Bone and the police agency's hired accountant, John Douglas. The interviews took place over five days in the RCMP detachment in north Toronto.

The similarity between these interviews and ones done nearly two years earlier by Wertheimer are striking. Wertheimer had instructed Gollogly to take each of the accounting binders in turn and don't look ahead. So, too, did Bone. Gollogly can be seen patiently explaining to both Wertheimer and Bone the rationale for each of the accounting entries he made in 2002 and 2003. He talked about the 303, the 189, the $80 million, the bonus payments.

Wertheimer left the hardest questions for her accountant. So, too, did Bone. And, just as was the case in January 2004, the longer the grilling continued, the gloomier Gollogly became. "They weren't listening," he confided later to a colleague.

When the RCMP began its investigation, the story line from Wilmer Cutler seemed like a pre-wrapped present, one that suited the times: Greedy executives had bent the rules to misrepresent the company's financial statements and trigger bonuses. The Wilmer Cutler gift included dozens of binders that purported to show how the accounting had not been done to U.S. GAAP. The outside investigators described a longstanding business culture they alleged was fine with the idea of manipulating the balance sheet.

But the deeper the RCMP and its accountants dug, the more difficult the terrain, the less clear the value of the package Wilmer Cutler had provided them. With the exception of Deloitte partners Bruce Richmond and Don Hathway no witness was remotely hostile to the accused. Mostly it was because they did not believe fraud had been committed. Nor did they agree with the accounting opinions offered by Wilmer Cutler and Huron Consulting.

Even the interviews involving Richmond and Hathway produced little of value for the prosecution. Richmond's anger was directed at Nortel's unwillingness to listen to some of his advice in 2003, such as delaying the filing of quarterly results until Wilmer Cutler had finished its work. But Richmond had been countermanded by audit committee chairman John Cleghorn, not the accused.

Nor did Hathway's evident hostility blind him to the accuseds' efforts to try to get Nortel's accounting right.

Consider this gem from the auditor's interview with the RCMP's Bone on Nov. 15, 2005 – nearly a year after Nortel published the summary of the findings of Wilmer Cutler:

"I thought they were doing a conscientious job," Hathway said, in reference to Gollogly and another colleague in Nortel's finance group. "They were making a concerted effort to respond to our questions and to get the right answers."

Hathway added he was surprised when Gollogly was fired.

Bone: OK. So you feel Mike (Gollogly) was doing a good job at trying to set the compliance, and scrub the balance sheet, and make the numbers right?

Hathway: At the time I did, I thought that.

Bone: What changed your opinion since that time?

Hathway: I'm not sure my opinion's changed.

This, from the Crown's angriest witness.

§

Dunn, Beatty and Gollogly had been eager to testify but their lawyers warned nothing but grief would attend that strategy. The Crown had only to prove fraud in excess of $5,000 to make its case – in a company the size of Nortel that was equivalent to stealing a pencil. Defence counsel worried Hubbard had enough experience to be able to trip up any one of the accused.

What surprised the defence, however, was how quickly the Crown's witnesses fell into their camp. The defence team had been prepared to introduce transcripts from RCMP and other interviews showing inconsistencies in testimony, but concluded early on this step wasn't necessary. Not one witness testified he or she had been asked to do anything wrong.

Starting with Brian Harrison, the defence strategy was to use each witness to introduce documents that explained how decisions had been made in 2002 and 2003 and how each of the line items on Nortel's general accounting ledger had been justified. Business records and emails from Nortel's finance group and Deloitte filled the electronic screens in the courtroom. Many of the electronic files, including the ones between Nortel and Deloitte, copied multiple employees and auditors. They showed very senior officials trying to fix problems, secure the paperwork for journal entries, prepare for audit committee presentations and meet statutory deadlines. The effect was cumulative, persuasive.

If there had been a conspiracy, as the Crown alleged, it had to have involved dozens – perhaps hundreds – of people. And, at the most senior levels, it would have included individuals who didn't like each other, who had no inclination to do favours for one another. As well, given the large numbers of checks and balances in Nortel's accounting system – with controllers double-checking entries from finance employees, and internal auditors trying to ensure the accounting was done according to industry standards – managing such a conspiracy would have been an extremely complex enterprise. It was beyond the capability of a company still recovering from a freefall.

A conspiracy made no sense.

12

The Letters That Went Unsent

Hubbard scoured the evidence for suspicious looking transactions and emails and highlighted these throughout the trial. Amid the wreckage of Nortel's downsizing, it wasn't difficult to find situations or accounting entries that fell outside the scope of what auditors might consider normal. These were not normal times for Nortel.

One of Hubbard's favourite examples of alleged malfeasance involved notes written but never delivered. In July 2003, Gollogly drafted a letter to three senior members of the board of directors, including chairman Red Wilson. In it, the controller detailed his frustration with Beatty and certain of his accounting transactions. Gollogly said he was prepared to accept being fired if the board did not see things his way. However, Gollogly never sent the letter – which was later discovered on his hard drive by Wilmer Cutler.

Hubbard spent a considerable amount of time on this, and a similar letter Gollogly drafted to Beatty. He maintained that each unsent letter confirmed that Nortel's financial statements were inaccurate, that the entries made by Beatty were improper, and that the manipulation of the accounts was material.

"Because Gollogly never sent his letter," Hubbard noted in his closing, "none of his knowledge of Nortel's quality of earnings was revealed to the public. This failure constituted a fraud on the public."

The reality was more complicated. Indeed, Judge Marrocco ruled that Nortel's audit committee was already aware of the various concerns outlined by Gollogly – with the exception of the entries made by Beatty, which in the end never made it into the financial statements.

Here's what happened. Late on July 10 or early July 11 Beatty met with Peter Dans, the company's director of financial planning, to review accounting items that still needed to be dealt with before the books were closed for the quarter ended June 30. Dans testified that he brought up the issue of the reserve that had been earlier set aside to cover future payments for the bonus program known as 'success.' Since the amounts to be paid out under the program varied according to Nortel's performance, the size of the reserve was adjusted quarterly.

Dans pointed out that Nortel was forecasting a smaller-than-expected profit, which meant that the 'success' reserve should be reduced by about $20 million. However, Gollogly was out of town attending to a family emergency. Beatty decided anyway to ask members of Gollogly's staff to make the adjustment to Nortel's general ledger (along with two other small items that offset each other in value). The effect was to transform a projected second-quarter net loss of $14 million into a net profit of $6 million, according to U.S. GAAP. (The transactions had no real impact on pro forma earnings – which were already positive, as well as being the key metric as far as bonuses were concerned.)

Gollogly was furious with the intervention. While he acknowledged in the letter that each of the three entries "could be argued on their own merits," the net effect was to create a profit "and I believe this was the sole intent of the action."

Beatty didn't see it that way. In the first place, he was Gollogly's superior and felt he had the right to make the entries. Secondly, while the transactions may have created a tiny GAAP profit, it translated into zero cents per share – the same as before. This is why Gollogly was less than categorical in his letter when he wrote that "these entries could be considered material."

Nevertheless, Gollogly's reaction to Beatty's intervention was forceful. Dunn was prompted to consult an outside lawyer who advised that in the post-Sarbanes-Oxley era, a CEO overrules his company controller at his peril. Let Gollogly win this argument, the lawyer suggested. Dunn accepted the advice. The entries were reversed on July 14, and never made it onto Nortel's official financial statements. Nortel reported a small second-quarter GAAP loss.

Gollogly also argued in his unsent letter to directors that executive bonuses should not be paid, even though Nortel had achieved pro forma profits in the second quarter. Gollogly wrote that the company had not returned to profitability "in the spirit under which I understand the return-to-profitability program was intended."

Pro forma earnings were strong in the second quarter, thanks to the inclusion of a couple of items totalling

$101 million involving one-time financial gains related to customer financing and other issues arising from contracts. Gollogly's issue was a philosophical one – he thought the return-to-profitability bonus should be tied more tightly to operations. Nevertheless, after making his objection known in person to a member of the audit committee, Gollogly accepted his bonus for the second quarter. Decisions about issuing bonuses were "above my pay grade," Gollogly decided later.

The tension between Gollogly and his colleagues Beatty and Dunn had been building for months – and not surprisingly.

By electing to concentrate on cleaning up Nortel's balance sheet as one of his top priorities, Gollogly inevitably found himself in the position of criticizing Beatty, his predecessor as controller, and Dunn, the former chief financial officer. It was on their watch that Nortel became a mergers machine, spending billions in company shares to acquire little-known startups such as Xros and Qtera. The emphasis was on speed, and hiring for the finance group tended to favour graduates with masters of business administration rather than degrees in staid, boring accounting.

When Nortel was breaking into new markets, Dunn looked to experts capable of putting together complex financing packages to encourage potential customers to purchase Nortel technology. But when the whole machine began moving in reverse Nortel's accounting apparatus buckled. There was a breakdown in systems and controls, exacerbated by the rapid loss of so many finance employees. It was why the company wound up with so many liabilities for which paperwork could not be found. It was the reason Gollogly was so keen to return the financial statements to a semblance of normality.

The physical distance between Gollogly and his two more senior colleagues did little to encourage a meeting of minds. The offices of Dunn and Beatty were in the north wing of the Brampton headquarters, easily a 10-minute walk from Gollogly's centre of operations. Complicating things, one of Gollogly's closest office neighbours was Deloitte auditor Hathway – whom Dunn disliked intensely.

Part of the animus was rooted in deep disputes over accounting issues. Dunn and Hathway argued over the meaning of 'probable' in establishing contingent liabilities – a rather fundamental dispute given Nortel's huge balance of accrued liabilities. Under Dunn's interpretation (and that of Deloitte for many decades) Nortel recorded a reserve if there was a 51-per-cent chance the future costs would be incurred. Hathway believed the probability should be set between 65 per cent and 80 per cent.

Dunn and Hathway also differed over the treatment of a significant tax asset – Hathway's advice, which was ignored, would have caused Nortel to breach covenants on its large debt. The arguments had nothing to do with allegations of fraud. In these and other cases, the source of friction was Hathway's tendency to adopt a different position from that of his predecessor, Mitch Scorcsik.

Given all the issues he was facing as he battled to keep Nortel alive, Dunn never forgave Hathway for making his job more difficult than it needed to be. Indeed, Dunn led the push late in 2003 to have Hathway replaced as auditor on the Nortel file, something Deloitte was in the process of doing when Wilmer Cutler arrived on the scene.

Hathway would outlast Dunn at Nortel and would later be relied upon by the Crown to testify against the former CEO. But not even he could lay a glove on Dunn, Beatty or Gollogly. Hathway's key contribution as a

Crown witness was to explain why Deloitte signed off on multiple sets of Nortel's books. The reason, Hathway said, was because Wilmer Cutler made it clear to him that he had been misled by Nortel employees during the first restatement. Just which employees, however, Hathway wouldn't say.

Instead, Hathway castigated several former Deloitte colleagues for not understanding their file or for making the wrong decisions. Among them were the three auditors who prepared the memo about why the release of $80 million in liabilities in the first quarter of 2003 was correct. Marrocco was unimpressed by Hathway's testimony.

"I find the memo persuasive," the judge ruled, noting that Hathway reviewed the memo at the time it was prepared and, further, did not offer an explanation during trial as to why he believed the math offered by De Acetis and her colleagues was wrong. "I reject Mr. Hathway's evidence to the effect that the calculations or conclusions in this draft memo are not correct."

After defence counsel Porter introduced the Deloitte memo on Feb. 2, Hubbard consulted his colleagues outside the courtroom. One leaned over to whisper, just loud enough to be overheard: "Well, there goes the $80 million," he said, "but at least we still have the fourth quarter."

13

Fourth-quarter Callout

The latter stages of the trial offered an odd spectacle. The Crown's allegations about cookie jars and its theory about the release of accruals to create profits in 2003 had been discredited by the evidence. So Hubbard responded in two ways. First, he simply repeated his allegations about how the accused manipulated earnings in 2003. Then he devoted enormous effort into trying to prove they had orchestrated a loss during the fourth quarter of 2002.

On one level, of course, the latter assertion made no sense. Nortel's board of directors had implemented a return-to-profitability program under which bonuses would be paid to all staff when the company began generating profits again – starting with the fourth quarter. The incentive was there not to intervene.

The Crown made much of the fact that Dunn had publicly predicted Nortel would record a fourth-quarter loss, and alleged he manipulated the results so that they would conform to his earlier projection. But again, the incentive for him to have done so just wasn't there – no CEO is going to be embarrassed at having to report a profit to his board of directors rather than a loss that had been forecast.

What Hubbard liked about the fourth-quarter numbers, however, was the suggestion of earnings manipulation, even if it was to produce a loss.

This is the Crown's version of events: On Jan. 6, 2003, senior finance managers gathered to consider the fourth-quarter results as they were shaping up. Brian Harrison, the manager in charge of forecasting, reported that the numbers were coming in better than expected – Nortel was likely to record a $73-million profit compared to the $100-million loss that had been suggested by his calculations just a few weeks earlier.

Hubbard alleged that Harrison was tasked to call Nortel's regional managers for additional accrued liabilities – with the result that head office received $176 million in late entries. This, in turn, restored the fourth-quarter loss.

But the trial would show that Nortel's finance managers were right to question whether Harrison had his numbers right. Under the still-dire economic circumstances at the time, his profit forecast didn't seem to make sense. It turned out Harrison had made two significant errors – a $59-million item involving revenue and a $50-million liability connected to 360 Networks, a telecom carrier that was suing Nortel. Had Harrison included these in his initial assessment, he would have forecast a loss.

Nevertheless, Hubbard tried to show the accounting transactions solicited by Harrison were improper. The Crown attorney was unsuccessful, despite the fact that some of these entries had a very odd feel to them. The common feature of these transactions was a mind-numbing complexity that allowed for multiple interpretations of motive. But once the full story became known, it was clear no crime had been committed.

The most bizarre item came to a head just two days before Nortel was to issue a press release showing a $62-million loss for the fourth quarter ended 2002. Nortel's finance group and Deloitte auditor Mitch Szorcsik determined the firm should have recognized an additional $25.5-million loss arising from one aspect of the sale of Nortel's optical components business to Bookham Technology in November 2002.

Nortel had bought the plant in 2001 from JDS. The terms allowed Nortel to reduce the $2.8-billion purchase price provided it relied on JDS for a certain percentage of its optical components until 2003. Under advice from Deloitte, Nortel applied a purchase discount. As long as it met its commitment to buy JDS components, Nortel would record a $42-million increase in its net quarterly income – which recognized a portion of the discount on the purchase price.

However, the original rationale for the accounting began to produce some rather odd results as the market for optical components collapsed. For one thing, the price Nortel paid for the property now looked wildly inflated, which meant that so, too, was the value of the purchase discount. When Nortel was recording multibillion-dollar losses in 2001 and 2002, none of this really mattered – the accounting wasn't material. But late in 2002, Nortel could contemplate breaking even again. Suddenly, the quarterly purchase discounts began to look very significant. Indeed, a member of Gollogly's staff calculated that this single item could account for most of Nortel's projected profits for 2003.

When Bookham acquired the JDS plant on Nov. 8, 2002, Gollogly decided it would be a good time to revisit the accounting – and Deloitte agreed. Working through the associated accounting policies was time-consuming. It took Gollogly and Szorcsik until Jan. 21 to finalize the decision to reverse $25.5 million of the $42 million that had already been recorded on the general ledger for the fourth quarter. The amount reversed corresponded to the period of Bookham ownership during that period.

However, rather than adding $25.5 million to the $62-million loss Nortel was already set to announce, the company booked an identical, offsetting gain of $25.5 million by adjusting its assumption about how much inventory was obsolete. This, too, was at the last minute. The result was that the quarterly loss stayed at $62 million.

Hubbard claimed the transaction was a prime example of improper earnings manipulation.

He noted in his opening statement that Nortel had booked nearly $1 billion worth of liabilities in connection with inventories that were excess or obsolete. "Because (these) accounts were huge and it was difficult to determine inventory's true value, the account's amounts could be easily manipulated," he told the court. "The accused resorted to these accounts as a cookie jar to hit earnings targets," he added.

Hubbard also noted that Nortel, under guidance from Wilmer Cutler and a new Deloitte opinion, later changed its accounting for the JDS transaction. Deloitte determined in the second restatement that the purchase price discount was worth $500 million and that the cost of buying the JDS plant should therefore have been reduced upfront by the same amount. This eliminated the need for quarterly adjustments in income at Nortel. Hubbard's view was that the second restatement was proof the original accounting was false.

Judge Marrocco disagreed emphatically. "Describing the original JDS entries as false or wrong inaccurately characterizes what occurred and could easily lead to the false conclusion that something inappropriate happened when the original accounting was done," he wrote in his 2013 judgment. "A consideration of the details of this transaction illustrates why it is impossible to draw the inference which the Crown urges from the fact that accounting entries are restated. The accounting for this transaction was changed because Deloitte changed its mind."

Even the circumstances surrounding the last-minute offset proved rather benign. Mezon, the assistant controller at the time, noted that the demands on Nortel's accountants had been exceptional. Her staff had worked huge amounts of overtime in order to prepare a very complex set of financial results, and had been set to release them.

"The purpose of the offset was so we didn't have to change all the documents," Mezon said.

Ken Crosson – the manager in charge of the excess and obsolete inventory file – ultimately approved the last-minute change. Mezon testified that Crosson had assured her he was able to justify it.

Of all Nortel's businesses, optical products had been damaged the most during the telecom crash. That is why it wound up with nearly $1 billion in excess and obsolete gear – and, late in 2002, new orders were still drying up quickly. In December, internal Nortel studies suggested it might be appropriate to increase the E&O provision by $50 million. Crosson passed along this possibility to Harrison who was preparing fourth-quarter forecasts.

Determining the value of the inventory involved the use of complicated algorithms that assessed the age of the equipment, the market segment, and how much various buyers were willing to pay for the gear. Late in December, Crosson decided to concentrate his limited resources on selling his inventory rather than reevaluating it. He opted for the moment to keep the E&O provision where it was.

However, when Harrison called him in the first week of January to ask if he had missed any accruals, Crosson had no trouble justifying an increase of up to $35 million in his E&O exposure. This was later adjusted to $30 million, then – in order to accommodate the JDS offset of $25.5 million – to $5 million.

Mezon testified that she and her colleagues had determined the $25.5-million transaction wasn't material – that is, significant to earnings. "If it had been, I would have looked at it more closely," she said.

At the time, Nortel had roughly 4.3 billion shares outstanding, which meant that the last-minute adjustment to earnings amounted to little more than half a penny per share. And whether the entry had been made or not, Nortel would have posted a small loss for the quarter.

Mezon added that she did one other thing: "I made sure the auditors knew." Defence lawyer Porter entered an exhibit showing that Deloitte approved the entry.

The decision to book an identical $25.5-million offset to avoid more paperwork was born of exhaustion. To suggest, as the Crown did, that this was evidence of earnings manipulation seemed a stretch. If Dunn and his colleagues were really conducting a criminal conspiracy, they would at least have tried to cover their tracks by using less obvious accounting entries.

Marrocco spent a lot of time analyzing this and other fourth-quarter accounting transactions brought to his attention by Hubbard. During Hubbard's final summation, the judge appeared to be taking dead aim at the issues involved in the JDS and E&O offset entries, as well as a similarly complex piece of accounting involving Perot Systems.

On at least eight occasions, Marrocco tried to clarify whether the motivation of the defendants mattered if the accounting involved a range of legitimate options. He wanted to know how Hubbard viewed a finance employee who was being asked to increase an accrual in a situation where there is no single correct answer in accounting terms.

"There's actually a range of values that you could assign," the judge suggested, "so in response to that request, you move the marker from where you had it to some other place within that range. I'm trying to understand whether that's acceptable or unacceptable in terms of your submission."

Hubbard didn't answer the question directly. Instead he highlighted the arbitrary nature of the decisions at Nortel. "Here's the number, I don't care how you get to it, just get to it and make up stuff to justify it," he said, describing the alleged mindset of Nortel's employees.

The judge interjected: "But there's a difference between making up something or recording something as false, creating an accrual that doesn't exist.

But if the accrual expense lies within a range of numbers and you're inside that range ... is that OK, notwithstanding the fact that it's motivated by a desire to meet some pre-determined target?"

One of Hubbard's Crown colleagues, David Friesen, was attuned to the potential weakness in the Crown's case. "Any particular accrual might withstand audit scrutiny viewed in isolation," he allowed, "but without an understanding of the earnings management process that's taking place, you're missing essential information."

Friesen was referring to the accounting that took place during the fourth quarter of 2002, but Hubbard had earlier emphasized that the Crown's case hung on the existence of a wider fraud. The Crown's closing statement alleged its first 10 witnesses – all senior Nortel managers – were "accomplices or participants to the fraud."

Hubbard elaborated: "So (the) Crown isn't expecting a case of this nature to call people to say Mr. Dunn told me to commit fraud," he said. "Everybody just knows what to do. They've been doing it for years."

Hubbard then returned to the theme of how accounting decisions at Nortel were guided by a desire to achieve bonus targets. "Is that just accident, error, or is it deliberate?" he asked rhetorically.

The judge interceded. "I hate to belabour that, but if you assume it's deliberate," Marrocco said, "do you not still have to go back and look at the actual release to determine whether that release was appropriate or not?"

"Well, it wasn't. It was restated," Hubbard replied.

"No, the conclusion about whether it's appropriate or not is a different question," the judge said. "I'm asking you whether or not it's the genuineness of that, the correctness of that release, which really controls whether it was appropriate or not, not what the intent was."

Marrocco answered his own question this way in his judgment: "Mr. Crosson, in my view, was responding to requests from his superiors," the judge wrote, "but I am not satisfied that he responded in an inappropriate way." Marrocco went on to suggest that a civil regulator such as the Ontario Securities Commission could have an issue with the means used to reach the final number. "(Crosson) indicated in his estimation there was some flexibility concerning excess and obsolete accrued liability balances relating to inventory," Marrocco wrote. "While his responses arguably were not entirely consistent with U.S. GAAP and while that may be a concern for securities regulators, the accrual balances which he agreed to increase could be changed without distorting Nortel's underlying financial reality." Crosson was guilty of no crime, in other words, and even the possibility of a civil transgression is debatable.

Revealingly, Hubbard called on few people with real perspective on Nortel's accounting, especially when it concerned entries made during the fourth quarter of 2002. The Crown attorney put only two Deloitte partners on the stand – Bruce Richmond, who had no responsibility for doing audits, and Hathway, the U.S. audit partner who was not assigned to the Nortel file until January 2003.

John Cawthorne, the most senior Deloitte audit partner, was the only one with signing authority for Nortel's books. He was the auditor who signed off on Nortel's fourth quarter, including the excess and obsolete inventory adjustments submitted by Crosson. Crucially, Cawthorne analyzed the liabilities that lacked paperwork and helped Nortel's accountants work through the associated issues.

Hubbard early in the trial had said he would call on Cawthorne to testify, but dropped him as a witness the day before he was scheduled to take the stand. On that day, it was defence counsellors who were upset by the move.

Equally revealing were other omissions in Hubbard's list of witnesses. He called no one from Nortel's group of internal auditors – the specialists consulted by company accountants for advice about whether entries conformed to constantly evolving rules as understood in U.S. GAAP. Nor did Hubbard bring to the stand the accounting experts relied upon by the Crown in determining whether Nortel's accounting met the appropriate standards.

The case depended heavily on no one poking holes in it.

14

Two Swings, Two Misses

The case on the surface seemed stronger on June 19, 2008 – the day the Integrated Market Enforcement Team laid charges. On the same day, the Toronto unit, which includes specialists from the RCMP, the Crown and the Ontario Securities Commission, charged six executives at Royal Group Technologies with fraud.

The timing was deliberate. The federal government launched IMET teams across the country in 2003 to signal its determination to deal with white-collar crime and the legal wars against former executives at Nortel and Royal Group were to have showcased the beginning of a new era for Canada's crime fighters.

"Cases like these send a very clear message that we're out there and we are cracking down and that the government is serious about attacking this type of criminal activity," declared Kevin Harrison, the head of the Toronto IMET.

IMET picked the wrong cases, however – not because they were difficult, but because no crimes had been committed.

Superficially, the Royal Group fight looked to be the easier one to win. The RCMP alleged several of the firm's senior executives, including CEO Vic De Zen, profited improperly when they bought a parcel of land in Vaughan West for $20.5 million in 1998 and sold it two-and-a-half months later to Royal Group's real estate arm for $27.4 million.

Following a six-month trial in 2010, Ontario Superior Court Justice Richard Blouin acquitted De Zen and his colleagues. He ruled they had acquired the property at a discount, added value during a rising property market and sold it at fair value. Blouin added there had been no attempt to conceal the transaction from the board of directors or company auditors.

So clear-cut was the evidence against fraud, Blouin rendered his verdict even before he delivered his written decision.

The Royal Group case in many ways turned out to be a revealing preview of the Nortel trial. For starters, the faces were familiar. Each of the accused in the Nortel proceeding hired counsel – David Porter, Gregory Lafontaine and Robin McKechney – who successfully defended individuals in the Royal Group case. Marrocco, then a litigator with the Toronto firm of Gowlings, had been involved through his representation of one of Royal Group's directors.

As would be the case in the 2012 trial of Nortel's finance executives, the witnesses did a lot of damage to the Crown that put them on the stand.

This is how Blouin summarized the Royal Group testimony: "The cross-examination in this case was largely focused on eliciting further evidence to complete the story as opposed to attacking witness credibility and reliability. I came to view the evidence presented as the Crown eliciting testimony which supported the absence of proper accounting and direct reporting, and the defence finding evidence from those same witnesses, which tended to show transparency and openness."

That is very much how the trial involving Dunn, Beatty and Gollogly played out, with the major exception that their lawyers inundated the Crown with documentary evidence. And they would have entered hundreds more documents had the Crown not declined at the last minute to produce promised witnesses.

§

How did it happen then? How did the Crown come to waste millions of dollars on a lost cause? Why was it so difficult for the former Nortel executives to shake this notion that they were dirty?

The outlines of the explanations are easier to see with the passage of time. The context was everything – Enron, Sarbanes-Oxley, the crushing loss of shareholder wealth at Nortel. All of these informed the decision-making at the time. There was a populist revolt against the excesses of the telecom bubble and the executives who contributed to it. The overseers at the SEC, the OSC and the U.S. Department of Justice made sure the boards of directors of publicly traded firms such as Nortel were not to interfere in their investigations. This stricture inhibited executives, auditors and other officials who might ordinarily have questioned investigators' methods and conclusions.

The nature of accounting contributed to the atmosphere of suspicion. Because so many of the costs on a corporate balance sheet and income statement are estimates, the profession allows for a degree of judgment that outsiders find puzzling, enough so to encourage thoughts of conspiracy. In the case of Nortel, independent professionals picked through the rubble of an epic restructuring, and developed a narrative that looked superficially plausible. The company's accountants – short-staffed and operating under extreme conditions – made mistakes. They also approved entries that pushed the company from a loss to a profit. But the accounting was legitimate.

Had criminal investigators done their own investigation from scratch, instead of relying on the work of Wilmer Cutler, they might well have determined long before trial that no crime had occurred. Alternatively, had Nortel's directors or auditors asked harder questions during Wilmer Cutler's investigation, they might have reached the same conclusion.

The sad part is, no one stepped up. The three who might have done so were cut loose, left to fend for themselves for nine years. They knew how close they had come to saving Canada's flagship technology firm – and how savagely that role had been taken away from them.

Epilogue

What Was Lost

It was sheer coincidence that Justice Warren Winkler began his potentially decisive mediation involving Nortel creditors on Jan. 14, 2013. It was the same day that charges were dismissed in the criminal trial involving Frank Dunn, Douglas Beatty and Michael Gollogly. It was also the fourth anniversary of the day Nortel sought court protection from its creditors.

Winkler, the Chief Justice of Ontario, a specialist in labour law and mediation, had been meeting off and on with Nortel's main creditors for nine months, to no avail. The session that began Jan. 14 was billed as a last-ditch effort to resolve the remaining claims on Nortel's estate – from bond holders to pensioners.

The company's estate is sizeable. After its descent into bankruptcy, Nortel's directors sold the firm's operating businesses for roughly $3 billion. A consortium led by tech leviathan Apple Inc. shelled out another $4.5 billion in mid-2011 for most of Nortel's remaining patents. By yearend 2012, Nortel's coffers were bulging with $10 billion in cash – representing the proceeds from the sales of the patents and the businesses, as well as $2.3 billion remaining from what the firm had on hand when it entered bankruptcy.

However, set against these liquid assets was some $27 billion in claims from more than 1,000 creditors.

The job of settling just who should get what has been unusually complex. There are separate bankruptcy proceedings in Canada, the U.S. and Britain – reflecting Nortel's strong global reach. Most multinationals that enter bankruptcy have a centre of operations that predominates and takes control of the proceedings. Not so in Nortel's case. Although the corporation is headquartered in Canada, the biggest chunk of its revenues was generated in the U.S. It also had extensive operations in the U.K., thanks to its early-1990s acquisition of Standard Telephones and Cable Ltd. In other words, there were three roughly equal jurisdictions with a legitimate claim on the Nortel estate, and no real way under law of breaking the logjam.

Few were surprised when Winkler ended his final mediation efforts 10 days after they began. A few weeks later, in March, the judges in charge of the Canadian and U.S. bankruptcy proceedings agreed creditors should just fight it out in Canadian and U.S. courts. (The agreement dismissed a motion from the U.K. bankruptcy administrator to engage a private arbitrator.)

In the meantime, the judges have used their discretion to set aside small amounts of Nortel's cash to help former Nortel employees most in need. From early 2011 to yearend 2012, the courts paid $58 million in health and welfare benefits to about 8,150 pensioners and several hundred former employees on long- and short-term disability. Judges also approved about $850,000 for ex-Nortel workers facing particular hardship, and $3.4

million to 1,130 employees who had been sacked prior to mid-2010 without severance pay.

All of this is a pittance in comparison with the amounts claimed by many of Nortel's former executives for pension and pay owing. Ex-chief executives including John Roth, Frank Dunn and Mike Zafirovski have lodged claims each in excess of $10 million. If they succeed in making their case, their combined settlement would, of course, reduce the amounts available for less well-compensated former employees.

Dunn, Beatty and Gollogly each filed claims against Nortel in 2006 for wrongful dismissal. These actions were stayed by the company's move into bankruptcy but will now form part of the upcoming court battles that will determine how Nortel's remaining cash will be disbursed. In the wake of their acquittal in the criminal proceeding, the three have been trying to return to a normal life. But the experience of the past decade has left its mark.

None can rest easily until civil actions against them have been withdrawn or resolved. The U.S. Securities and Exchange Commission and the Ontario Securities Commission alleged in 2007 suits that the three former executives engaged in fraudulent accounting with respect to earnings and, in the case of Beatty and Dunn, with revenue as well. The proceedings had been on hold until the resolution of the criminal case. At the time of this writing, the SEC and OSC were still studying Judge Frank Marrocco's ruling.

§

In the weeks following Marrocco's judgment, each of the three executives headed south for a vacation. Beatty, who had seemed the most stressed throughout the yearlong trial, who had had the most difficulty sleeping the night before the judgment, did not return home for weeks. It was not guilt that had kept Beatty awake; it was the knowledge that even in the Canadian justice system, anything could happen. Marrocco was just one man, judge and jury, and a former prosecutor. Had he viewed some of the evidence through the same distorted prism as the Crown?

Beatty's uncertainty was also rooted in the long legal fight he and Dunn waged against Chubb Insurance to force the insurer to pay their lawyers' bills. The slugfest produced one surprise decision after another – it wasn't until early 2011 that Beatty knew he would have the resources to defend himself in his many other proceedings.

But even with this victory, the psychological pressure was immense. Beatty shared custody of two daughters. They were teenagers when their father was charged. When Marrocco exonerated Beatty, they were in their mid-twenties. Beatty did not encourage his daughters to attend the trial – he was sensitive about how the experience might affect them. The former CFO found a sense of normalcy outside the case by doing some accounting for a friend who runs a small financial services company in Toronto. He has also been assisting some startup companies.

The lengthy legal process has naturally hurt the defendants' ability to earn a living. As long as they continue to face civil sanctions, they are not permitted to serve with a public company.

Gollogly adapted by changing his role. He became a stay-at-home dad for his young daughter while his wife, Mary, continued her career in financial services. Indeed, Gollogly's lawyer Sharon Lavine successfully pleaded a motion to transfer the criminal trial from Oshawa to Toronto – so that the lengthy proceeding would not be an undue hardship.

Dunn's immediate family attended the trial off and on and provided more than just moral support. During the pretrial proceedings, when he was uncertain whether he could afford to see the legal battle through, Dunn enlisted his daughter Kelly – a lawyer – to help organize part of his defence. His victory over Chubb Insurance in 2010 helped Dunn's finances sufficiently to allow him to rely fully on his allies at McCarthy Tétrault.

It also allowed him to purchase a property on Florida's Gulf Coast, where he has been dividing his time between golf and preparing to take on the SEC, the OSC and the trustees of the Nortel estate in his wrongful dismissal suit.

Each of the accused spent years helping their lawyers sift through the millions of documents the case produced. But for Dunn it became an obsession.

He maintained a hard drive of data, cross-referenced the emails and trial exhibits and meticulously maintained a timeline of events from 2002 and beyond. Dunn undoubtedly drove his lawyers batty but it was also apparent they came to rely on his encyclopedic knowledge.

Had it not been for the stubbornness of the accused – their refusal to accept the narrative prepared by others – and their willingness to court personal bankruptcy in pursuit of justice, this story would have had a much different ending. Instead, they find themselves trying to cope with myriad conflicting emotions – from relief to rage – and wondering what they might have done differently with the decade each of them lost.

Timeline

The long road to justice for Nortel's financial executives

2002

Summer: Nortel establishes a management 'disclosure' committee in response to the passage of the Sarbanes-Oxley bill in the U.S. A group of eight or so executives meets weekly to determine appropriate responses to new governance rules.

August: CFO Douglas Beatty leads a companywide review of accrued liabilities. The Crown alleges that the analysis shows $303 million is no longer required and available for release into income. Later evidence would show most of the amount had already been properly removed from the balance sheet.

November: Nortel's board of directors approves a 'return to profitability' plan to award cash bonuses to all employees when Nortel achieves pro forma earnings.

2003

April 24: Nortel reports a first-quarter profit.

May 9: Nortel's external auditor Deloitte tells the audit committee "we are not aware of any material modifications that should be made."

July 24: Deloitte first informs the audit committee of deficiencies in documentary support for certain accruals on the balance sheet as of June 30. These had been brought to Deloitte's attention by Nortel's controller,

Michael Gollogly. Nortel initiates a review of assets and liabilities.

Oct. 23: Preliminary findings of the review show that the company has overstated liabilities by roughly $900 million U.S. Nortel revises financial statements accordingly.

Nov. 18: Nortel's audit committee hires Washington-based Wilmer Cutler Pickering Hale and Dorr LLP as part of an independent review into the circumstances that led to the Oct. 23 restatement. Soon after, Beatty takes investigators through the history of the accounting.

Nov. 19: Nortel formally files a $952-million restatement with the U.S. Securities and Exchange Commission.

December: Beatty meets in Washington with SEC officials to explain the restatement.

2004

Jan. 7: Wilmer Cutler begins interviewing Nortel executives, starting with Beatty, who is also questioned on Jan. 9 and again late in April just before he was fired.

Jan. 21: Wilmer Cutler completes third and final interview with Gollogly.

Jan. 29: Nortel issues fourth-quarter results showing profits. The top 16 executives, excluding Frank Dunn and Beatty, are awarded restricted stock units worth $27.3 million under a longer-term bonus plan.

Feb. 19: Wilmer Cutler conducts first interview with Dunn.

March 10: Beatty and Gollogly update members of Nortel's audit committee. The presentation shows documentation for issues of concern to Wilmer Cutler has been forwarded to Deloitte, Nortel's external auditor. However, Gollogly reveals that $300 million worth of additional liabilities, not captured in the first restatement, may lack paperwork thanks to the brutal downsizing of the firm. Nortel reveals that it may have to revise the restatement made in October.

March 15: Beatty and Gollogly are placed on paid leave pending the completion of the audit committee's work. Nortel appoints Bill Kerr as chief financial officer and MaryAnne Pahapill as controller on an interim basis.

March 16: Michael McMillan, Nortel's director of consolidations, sends Wilmer Cutler a detailed synopsis of the accounting related to the first restatement.

March 17: A shareholder class-action lawsuit is filed against Nortel. This would eventually be settled with Nortel paying $575 million in cash and billions more in shares.

March 21: Wilmer Cutler interviews Dunn a second and final time, but this time his lawyers participate. Later, the lawyers would be forced to testify at trial.

March 29: Kerr gives a presentation to Nortel's board showing that most of the alleged $303-million 'cookie jar' never existed.

April 27: Nortel fires Dunn, Beatty and Gollogly 'for cause.' Board member Bill Owens is appointed CEO.

Late April: Nortel's accounting difficulties trigger separate investigations by the Ontario Securities Commission and the SEC.

May: The U.S. Attorney for the Northern District of Texas begins a criminal investigation of Nortel's accounting. The RCMP starts its probe around the same time. The U.S. decides early in 2008 not to pursue criminal charges.

2005

Jan. 11: Nortel releases a second restatement of revenue and earnings, along with a summary of a report by Wilmer Cutler that concluded that Nortel's finance group had manipulated liabilities to produce desired earnings in 2002 and early 2003. Nortel's audit committee launches a review of the circumstances, leading eventually to a third restatement.
January: Nortel files claims against Dunn, Beatty and Gollogly, seeking the return of payments made to them under the company's bonus plans.

2006

Feb. 8: Nortel announces the settlement of seven class-action lawsuits in Canada and the U.S. by agreeing to pay shareholders $575 million in cash and 62.9 million shares. (The agreement is finalized March 20, 2007.)
March 10: Nortel says it will restate its financial numbers for the third time after the audit committee's review alleges the firm's finance group had improperly accounted for revenues in contracts that contained multiple commitments to customers. Dunn and his colleagues say the accounting was according to the rules.
April: Dunn files a claim against Nortel for wrongful dismissal, defamation and mental stress.
May: Gollogly files a similar claim.
October: Beatty files a similar claim.

2007

March 1: Nortel says it will restate its financial numbers for a fourth time.
March 12: The SEC files civil fraud charges against Dunn, Beatty, Gollogly and Pahapill. It alleges Dunn,

Beatty and Pahapill altered Nortel's revenue recognition policies to accelerate revenue as needed to meet forecasts, and from at least July 2002 to June 2003, Dunn, Beatty and Gollogly improperly established, maintained and released reserves to meet earnings targets. The financial executives say they did not contravene accounting rules.

March 12: The OSC issues a notice of hearing to consider orders to apply a variety of penalties to Dunn, Beatty and Gollogly.

March 27: The OSC publishes a statement of allegations asserting that Dunn, Beatty and Gollogly authorized, permitted or acquiesced in making material misstatements in filings to the OSC. The executives deny they did anything improper.

May 22: The OSC approves a settlement with Nortel under which the firm agrees to keep the OSC apprised of its progress in fixing accounting and related issues. Nortel agrees to pay $1 million to help cover the cost of the OSC investigation.

Sept. 12: The SEC charges four more former Nortel officers with accounting fraud – Douglas Hamilton, Craig Johnson, James Kinney and Kenneth Taylor.

Oct. 15: The SEC files civil fraud charges against Nortel, alleging the firm engaged in accounting fraud from 2000 to 2003 to close gaps between its true performance and internal targets and/or Wall Street expectations. Without admitting or denying the charges, Nortel settles with the SEC by consenting to pay a $35-million civil penalty which the SEC will place in a Fair Fund to distribute to affected shareholders.

2008

Early 2008: The assistant U.S. Attorney for the Northern District of Texas decides not to pursue a criminal case against Nortel's executives.

April 30: The SEC announces that Johnson, Kinney and Taylor (vice-presidents of finance, respectively, for Nortel's wireline, wireless and enterprise business units) agreed to settle the charges against them arising from their alleged involvement in Nortel's earnings management fraud during 2002 and 2003. Each pays fines of $75,000 and other penalties. Hamilton and Pahapill continue to fight the allegations.

May 6: The RCMP asks Nortel to redisclose its main documents so it can create a searchable database. Only 200,000 of four million documents had been imported into the RCMP's document management system by this date.

June 19: The RCMP announces criminal charges against Dunn, Beatty and Gollogly alleging fraud affecting the public market, falsification of books and documents, and false prospectus. The three executives deny the charges.

2009

Jan. 14: Nortel files for bankruptcy protection.

Sept. 3: The SEC's case against Dunn, Beatty, Gollogly and others is stayed pending the resolution of Canadian criminal proceedings.

Oct. 29: The SEC creates a Fair Fund, totalling $35.5 million, consisting of payments by Nortel, Johnson, Kinney and Taylor. A court-approved plan of distribution to investors is finalized on Oct. 5, 2011. It covers purchases of Nortel common shares from Oct. 24,

2000 to Feb. 15, 2001 and/or April 24, 2003 to April 27, 2004.

Dec. 21: Judge Cary Boswell rules the Crown must make a proper disclosure of Nortel's documents to the three accused.

2010

Jan. 28: The Crown amends its fraud charges against Dunn, Beatty and Gollogly, pushing back the start of the relevant period from Jan. 1, 2002 to Jan. 1, 2000. The move triggers a clause in Nortel's insurance coverage more favourable to the accused.

April 23: Judge Donald Cameron rules that Chubb Insurance should bear 90 per cent of the legal costs incurred by Dunn, Beatty and Gollogly.

September: The trial venue is changed from Oshawa to Toronto.

2011

Jan. 18: The Ontario Court of Appeal upholds Cameron's ruling: Dunn, Beatty and Gollogly will have their legal costs covered by Chubb.

July 1: Nortel reaches a deal to sell the last of its assets.

2012

Jan. 16: The criminal trial against Dunn, Beatty and Gollogly begins in Toronto. The Crown leads 17 witnesses through to June 26.

Feb. 2: Defence attorney David Porter introduces a Deloitte memo that undercuts the Crown's theory the accused had practised cookie jar accounting to trigger bonuses.

Feb. 17: Porter enters a second key memo showing that Deloitte had been working with Nortel to figure out the proper accounting for more than $400 million worth of liabilities that lacked paperwork. It shows the accused had been trying to get the numbers right.
Aug. 3: The Crown files final written arguments.
Sept. 14: The defence files final written arguments.
Sept. 27, 28: Crown's final oral arguments.
Oct. 2, 3: Final oral arguments from the defence.

2013

Jan. 14: Ontario Superior Court Justice Frank Marrocco dismisses all charges.
Feb. 12: The Crown declines to appeal.

Frank Dunn (left), the chief financial officer, took over as Nortel's CEO from John Roth in November 2001. The executives were eight months into what would become one of the biggest downsizings in Canadian corporate history – 60,000 Nortel jobs would disappear in less than two years.
[Credit: Nortel handout]

William McLucas, a partner with Washington-based law firm Wilmer Cutler Pickering Hale and Dorr, was approached in 2003 by Nortel's audit committee to provide a second opinion on Nortel's $952-million restatement. He queried Nortel's finance executives in 'an aggressive tone.'
[Credit: Susan B. Markisz/National Post]

Laura Wertheimer, who joined Wilmer Cutler in 2003, ran the independent investigation of Nortel's financial statements. It was her first assignment with her new firm, one she approached with zeal.
[Credit: WilmerHale, formerly Wilmer Cutler Pickering Hale and Dorr]

John Cleghorn was chairman of Nortel's audit committee. The former CEO of the Royal Bank of Canada hired the investigators from Wilmer Cutler and followed their work closely. He instructed Wilmer Cutler to stay away from the working files of Deloitte – Nortel's independent auditor.
[Credit: Matthew Sherwood/National Post]

Nortel's chairman, Red Wilson, was the longest-serving member of the board and played a key role in convincing Frank Dunn to take on the role of CEO in 2001 when it seemed no one else wanted the job. He presented Dunn with a line drawing on Feb. 25, 2004, as thanks for 'saving the company.' Two months later, Wilson fired him.]
[Credit: Peter J. Thompson/National Post]

Mike Zafirovski (right) took over Nortel's top job from
Bill Owens (background) on Oct. 17, 2005. Zafirovski, a
former Motorola executive, would preside over Nortel's
descent into bankruptcy protection in 2009. While
experienced businessmen, neither was deeply familiar
with the telecommunications equipment industry.
[Credit: Norm Betts/Bloomberg News]

Frank Dunn and his wife, Nancy, leave the Newmarket courthouse on June 19, 2008 – the day the former CEO was charged with accounting fraud. It would be another four-and-a-half years before he and his colleagues saw the charges dismissed.
[Credit: Brett Gundlock/National Post]

The finished version of the Oakville mansion once owned by Frank Dunn. Dunn was forced to sell the property after he was fired in 2004. His proceeds were about $9 million, but his legal bills were extensive. He borrowed from friends a few years later to fund his criminal defence.
[Credit: theinvidiatateam.com]

Robert Hubbard led the case for the Crown. He was assisted by Amanda Rubaszek (background left). Hubbard's theatrical gestures in the courtroom – along with his constant allegations of impropriety – had the accused gritting their teeth.
[Credit: Michelle Siu/National Post]

Jeff Ansley was Assistant U.S. Attorney for the Northern
District of Texas in 2008, when he decided not to pursue
a criminal case against Nortel's top financial executives.
Ansley opted out after interviewing a key member of
Nortel's accounting group in the U.S.
[Credit: Bell Nunnally & Martin LLP]

Ontario Superior Court Justice Frank Marrocco, seen
here in 2005 when he was a partner at Gowlings. His
civility and dry wit were evident throughout the yearlong
trial.
[Credit: Peter Redman/National Post]

Lead defence attorney David Porter (centre) gives a brief statement Jan. 14, 2013, following the not guilty ruling by Judge Frank Marrocco. The soft-spoken corporate lawyer was not comfortable with the media and not inclined to challenge the Crown's witnesses when he didn't have to. He won by piling up a mountain of evidence either ignored or misinterpreted by the Crown. [Credit: Darren Calabrese/National Post]

Deloitte auditor Don Hathway was considered the
Crown witness most hostile to the accused. But even he
felt they had been trying to get the numbers right.
Hathway's testimony was followed closely in the
courtroom by a phalanx of Deloitte lawyers.
[Credit: James Bagnall/Ottawa Citizen]

Nortel's top U.S. accountant, Karen Sledge, surprised Michael Gollogly – Nortel's controller – with new estimates for fringe benefit costs. When Gollogly urged her to redo her math, Wilmer Cutler's investigators saw it as a sign of earnings manipulation. The trial would show otherwise.
[Credit: James Bagnall/Ottawa Citizen]

Michael Gollogly exits the courthouse on Jan. 14, 2013, in Toronto after learning he had been acquitted of all charges. In the years leading up to the trial, he was a stay-at-home dad for his young daughter.
[Credit: Darren Calabrese/National Post]

Douglas Beatty reacts after the charges were dismissed
on Jan. 14, 2013. The relief was not total. He and his
colleagues must still wait to see whether civil charges –
stayed for the criminal case – will be withdrawn in light
of the evidence presented in court.
[Credit: Michelle Siu/The Canadian Press]

After the charges were dismissed, Frank Dunn
celebrated over dinner, quietly, with his family. He and
his wife, Nancy, then headed to Florida. Dunn is waging
a wrongful dismissal suit against the Nortel estate as
well as pushing the Ontario Securities Commission and
its U.S. equivalent to withdraw civil fraud charges.
[Credit: Darren Calabrese/National Post]

Nortel's retirees have been waiting more than four years to learn what their former employer's bankruptcy means for their pensions. Major claimants were ordered early in 2013 to prepare for a final court battle to determine how Nortel's $10-billion estate will be divided amongst $27 billion worth of claims.
[Credit: Wayne Cuddington/Ottawa Citizen]

Made in the USA
Columbia, SC
08 March 2020